REVEALING PEARLS & DIAMONDS

Commentary on Selected Duas of
Rasulullah ﷺ

Dr. M. Yunus Kumek

Cover and Chapter Photos: Courtesy of Artist Muhammad McMillan

Medina House
publishing

www.medinahouse.org
170 Manhattan Ave, PO Box 63
New York 14215
contact@medinahouse.org

ISBN 978-1-950979-03-5

Published in the United States of America.

Dedicated to the Lives like
Kelly and Andrew of Williamsville, New York,
Paul (just received a phone text today that he passed away in an accident-09/28/19) and Mark of Kalamazoo, Michigan, A. Ahad of Istanbul-New York, O(u)sman(e)s of Buffalo, NY & Boston, MA

To the Memories and Hopes that (inshAllah) John Burkhart (d.2017) of Iowa-New York, Sh. Sulub Kahin of Somali-New York (d.2016) and Selim Sasati (d.1998), Uncle Celal-Lale Yenge-Aunt Safiye-Little Boy Ensar (lost their lives in the earthquake, d.1999) and Buyukbaba (Grandpa, d.1995)—Buyukanne (Grandma, d.2001) of Istanbul are ok as they finished their journey in this life ...

CONTENTS

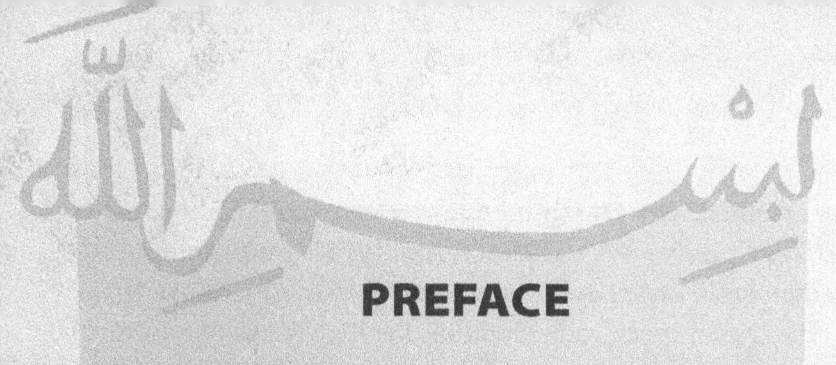

PREFACE

بِسْمِ اللهِ الرَّحْمَنِ الرَّحِيمِ
الْحَمْدُ للهِ رَبِّ الْعَالَمِينَ
اَللّٰهُمَّ صَلِّ عَلَى سَيِّدِنَا وَحَبِيبِنَا وَمَوْلَانَا مُحَمَّدٍ

وَمَا أَرْسَلْنَاكَ إِلَّا رَحْمَةً لِّلْعَالَمِينَ {الأنبياء/107}

And We have not sent you, [Oh Muhammad!], except as a mercy to the worlds, [1] [Anbiya:107].

وَمَا أَرْسَلْنَاكَ إِلَّا كَافَّةً لِّلنَّاسِ بَشِيرًا وَنَذِيرًا وَلَكِنَّ أَكْثَرَ النَّاسِ لَا يَعْلَمُونَ {سبأ/28}

And We have not sent you except comprehensively to mankind as a bringer of good tidings and a warner. But most of the people do not know [1] [Saba:28].

Rasulullah ﷺ [1] was the embodiment of humility and humbleness with the embodiment of gratitude and gratefulness to Allah سبحانه وتعالى essentially, and to the creation as the reflection of this

1. Rasulullah ﷺ: The word Rasulullah can be translated as "the Messenger or Prophet of Allah." Rasulullah in its usage is the Prophet *Muhammad (peace and blessings be upon him). The Arabic writing* ﷺ is read as "Sallallahu alayhi wa sallam" abbreviated as "saws" when the name of the Prophet Muhammad is mentioned. This expression is practically and commonly translated as *"peace and blessings be upon him"*. The expressions ﷺ or saw(s) are expressions and phrases of blessings, peace and respect for the Prophet Muhammad when his name is mentioned. There are also expressions and phrases of blessings and peace used for the other Prophets of Allah such as Abraham, Moses, and Jesus and others.

core essential. The Quran mentions about Rasulullah ﷺ as: وَمَا أَرْسَلْنَاكَ إِلَّا رَحْمَةً لِّلْعَالَمِينَ {الأنبياء/107}, *And We have not sent you, [Oh Muhammad!], except as a mercy to the worlds,* [1] [Anbiya:107].

The Quran specifically mentions the high status of Rasulullah ﷺ embodying this role model for all creation. The position of this exemplary perfect embodiment of Rasulullah ﷺ is for all humans as mentioned in the Quran وَمَا أَرْسَلْنَاكَ إِلَّا كَافَّةً لِّلنَّاسِ بَشِيرًا وَنَذِيرًا {سبأ/28}, *And We have not sent you except comprehensively to mankind as a bringer of good tidings and a warner,*" [1] [Saba:28].

One of the examples of this embodiment is through the engagements of dua[2]. In this regard, this book tries to reveal this very critical robust dynamics behind the mere or simple looking words. The transliterations of the original Arabic duas are presented in the footnotes as well in order to engage non-Arabic readers with the original sounds of these prayers. Yet, they are the pearls and diamonds and but one should try to uncover, think, realize, understand, appreciate and use them regularly but yet, we seem not to understand it as mentioned وَلَكِنَّ أَكْثَرَ النَّاسِ لَا يَعْلَمُونَ {سبأ/28}, *but most of the people do not know and understand,* [1] [Saba:28].

May Allah سبحانه وتعالى make us to realize about this noble position of Rasulullah ﷺ and truly appreciate all his teachings including his duas[3].

اَللّٰهُمَّ صَلِّ عَلٰى سَيِّدِنَا وَحَبِيبِنَا وَمَوْلَانَا مُحَمَّدٍ

Dr. Muhammad Yunus Kumek
August 2, 2019
Lecturer on Muslim Ministry & Spiritual Care
Fall 2019
Harvard Divinity School

2. Dua is singular translated as "prayer."
3. Duas with added "s" is plural translated as "prayers."

NEED FOR EXPLANATION OF DUAS

قُل مَا يَعْبَأُ بِكُمْ رَبِّي لَوْلَا دُعَاؤُكُمْ فَقَدْ كَذَّبْتُمْ فَسَوْفَ يَكُونُ لِزَامًا {الفرقان/77}

SAY [unto those who believe]: "No weight or value would my Sustainer attach to you were it not for your dua [prayer to Allah]!" And say unto those who deny the truth:] "You have indeed given the lie [to God's message], and in time this [sin] will cleave unto you!" (Furqan:77) [2].

The essence of the religion is dua. The essence of worship is dua [5]. The dua means the person's need for Allah[4] سبحانه وتعالى. This is the reality. Sometimes, we do not realize our reality. The pseudo or fake barriers prevent us from connecting with the Real Doer of everything, Who is Allah سبحانه وتعالى.

If Allah سبحانه وتعالى[5] was to turn away from the universe for even one second, the entire universe can be destructed or will certainly collapse. If a person does not turn to Allah سبحانه وتعالى, similarly the person will collapse and become destructed spiritually due to the lack of the real purpose of their existence in their hearts and

---

4. Allah is the Proper Name of the One and Only Unique Creator, with other numerous Names and Attributes, translated in English as God.
5. The expression سبحانه وتعالى read as Subhãnahu wa Tã'la also abbreviated as SWT and written also as Allah (SWT) is an expression of respect when the Name of Allah is mentioned. Among these expressions many English translations, one can be "Allah is One, Unique and Perfect with all the Divine Attributes and Names, far beyond human's negative and wrong constructions and imaginations. All Glory Belongs to Allah, the Most Exalted, the Most Respected, and the Most High.

souls, qalb and ruh. The body can still be alive yet, the person is dead as mentioned:

> أَفَلَمْ يَسِيرُوا فِي الْأَرْضِ فَتَكُونَ لَهُمْ قُلُوبٌ يَعْقِلُونَ بِهَا أَوْ آذَانٌ يَسْمَعُونَ بِهَا فَإِنَّهَا لَا تَعْمَى الْأَبْصَارُ وَلَكِن تَعْمَى الْقُلُوبُ الَّتِي فِي الصُّدُورِ {الحج/46}
>
> *Have they, then, never journeyed about the earth, letting their hearts gain wisdom, and causing their ears to hear? Yet, verily, it is not their eyes that have become blind—but blind have become the hearts that are in their breasts!* (Hajj:46) [2].

This is a reality and not an exaggeration. The more we learn and practice, the more we realize and embody this concept.

In this regard, anything that would minimize this heedlessness should help inshAllah. This book is an effort to reveal and uncover these duas of the Prophet [6]ﷺ that are valued as diamonds and pearls. Diamonds and pearls are only stones which gain value in the eyes of people. Therefore, we use these words to humanize the language. Yet, the duas of the Prophet ﷺ has the utmost value for Rabbul A'lamin[7], in connecting, communicating and expressing our real needs to Allah سبحانه وتعالى.

---

6. The Prophet ﷺ denotes the Prophet *Muhammad (peace and blessings be upon him)*. The Arabic writing ﷺ is read as "Sallallahu alayhi wa sallam" abbreviated as "saws" when the name of the Prophet Muhammad is mentioned. This expression is practically and commonly translated as "peace and blessings be upon him". The expressions ﷺ or saws are expressions and phrases of blessings, peace and respect for the Prophet Muhammad when his name is mentioned. There are also expressions and phrases of blessings and peace used for the other Prophets of Allah such as Abraham, Moses, and Jesus and others.

7. Another Name or Attribute for Allah, which can be translated as Sustainer and Nourisher of all worlds, and universes

Sometimes we don't realize these needs but Rasulullah [8] ﷺ teaches us. Saying and presenting these duas to Allah سبحانه وتعالى in our personal connection can be a step. Yet, there can always be the cases of people مَثَلُ الَّذِينَ حُمِّلُوا التَّوْرَاةَ ثُمَّ لَمْ يَحْمِلُوهَا كَمَثَلِ الْحِمَارِ يَحْمِلُ أَسْفَارًا بِئْسَ مَثَلُ الْقَوْمِ الَّذِينَ كَذَّبُوا بِآيَاتِ اللَّهِ وَاللَّهُ لَا يَهْدِي الْقَوْمَ الظَّالِمِينَ {الجمعة/5} who were given a noble guidance and revelation from Allah. Yet, this true guidance did not benefit them. Allah does not guide the people who are involved with evil and they reject the signs of Allah, (Jumu'a:5) [2].

However, the next step should be to understand what we present to Allah سبحانه وتعالى, then to realize all those expressed by the Prophet ﷺ really exist in us, then with this utmost realization and need, we make an effort to fully connect to Allah سبحانه وتعالى, Rabbul A'lamin with these masnun Duas, with tears, crying and begging. This connection should include tears, crying, and begging. Tears, crying and begging can be only the expressions or symbols of possible realization of these needs in us.

It is hoped that inshAllah, Allah سبحانه وتعالى will not turn us away empty handed with the Divine Fadl and Rahmah.

---

8. The Prophet *Muhammad (peace and blessings be upon him). The Arabic writing* ﷺ is read as "Sallahu alayhi wa salllam" abbreviated as "saws" when the name of the Prophet Muhammad is mentioned. The expressions ﷺ or saws are expressions and phrases of blessings and peace for the Prophet Muhammad. They are also the expressions and phrases of blessings and peace used for the other Prophets of Allah such as Abraham, Moses, and Jesus and others.

IMPORTANCE OF DUA IN HADITH

Each part of the dua of the Prophet ﷺ is very critical and one can write pages on its importance and application to one's daily life. As one can see, Rasulullah[9] ﷺ has short statements with very intensive, useful, convoluted, and deep meanings. The term 'Jawami al-Kalim'[10] is used for the quality of the words of Rasulullah [3] ﷺ to indicate the deep meanings in the simple looking statements.

This shows that the hadith itself is a revelation from Allah سبحانه وتعالى called gayru matluw. So, it is not, astagfirullah[11], a human is talking but it is another level of revelation to Rasulullah ﷺ at a human level as a mercy of Allah سبحانه وتعالى to us showing the practical and correct applications of the Quran in our lives.

---

9. Rasulullah ﷺ: The word Rasulullah can be translated as "the Messenger or Prophet of Allah." Rasulullah in its usage is the Prophet *Muhammad (peace and blessings be upon him). The Arabic writing* ﷺ is read as "Sallalahu alayhi wa sallam" abbreviated as "saws" when the name of the Prophet Muhammad is mentioned. This expression practically and commonly translated as "*peace and blessings be upon him*". The expressions ﷺ or saws are expressions and phrases of blessings, peace and respect for the Prophet Muhammad when his name is mentioned. There are also the expressions and phrases of blessings and peace used for the other Prophets of Allah such as Abraham, Moses, and Jesus and others.

10. Conciseness of speech. A few words with dense and convoluted meanings. This is a specific title given and used only for the Prophet Muhammad, Rasulullah ﷺ.

11. Oh Allah! Please forgive me!

Therefore, the common expressions one can hear in Jum'a Khutbahs[12] as "inna asdaqa al-hadisi kitabulllah, wa ahsanal huda, hadyi Muhammadin [3] [4] ﷺ [13]" mentioned originally by Rasulullah ﷺ. This statement is not a mere statement but rather a summarization of the authentic epistemology in Islam. In this regard, the usul, etiquette and methodology of authentic learning in Islam is:

1. Quran
2. Hadith
3. Qiyas (Analysis) & ijma (Consensus)

The above methodology has set the guidelines since the time of Rasulullah ﷺ and it is not going to change until the End of Days inshAllah.

Sometimes, we make the mistake of analyzing only the Quran and famous hadiths about the diligent issues of tawhid and iman. Yet, the duas of Rasulullah ﷺ should be analyzed in a similar diligence to deduce meanings especially with the changing times and generations emerging with issues depending on the culture, people and context. In this regard, the duas of Rasulullah ﷺ are very critical not only as the source of knowledge to revive these notions of tawhid and iman but also to apply them in one's life with a desperate need.

The Quran mentions [1]:

> قُلْ مَا يَعْبَأُ بِكُمْ رَبِّي لَوْلَا دُعَاؤُكُمْ فَقَدْ كَذَّبْتُمْ فَسَوْفَ يَكُونُ لِزَامًا {الفرقان/77} *Say, What would my Lord care for you if not for your supplication?" For you [disbelievers] have denied, so your denial is going to be adherent* (Furqan: 77).

---

12. Friday Sermons
13. The most truthful words are the Book of Allah, the Quran. The best guidance is the guidance of Rasulullah ﷺ.

This verse indicates that the value of a person can be revealed with sincere dua to Allah سبحانه وتعالى. Yet, it is a matter of question how much time we spend in our daily activities on dua. We regularly try to spend time reading the Quran and increasing our knowledge, Alhamdulillah. But the habit of taking the time to make dua, not just for a few minutes but rather for at least half an hour to an hour daily, unfortunately may not be a common habit, Allahu A'lam (Allah knows the best). May Allah سبحانه وتعالى forgive me and all of us and make us from the ones who sincerely connect to Allah سبحانه وتعالى with dua, Amin.

وَإِذَا سَأَلَكَ عِبَادِي عَنِّي فَإِنِّي قَرِيبٌ أُجِيبُ دَعْوَةَ الدَّاعِ إِذَا دَعَانِ فَلْيَسْتَجِيبُواْ لِي وَلْيُؤْمِنُواْ بِي لَعَلَّهُمْ يَرْشُدُونَ {البقرة/186}

And when My seekers, worshippers, and adorers ask you, [O Muhammad], concerning Me—indeed I am near. I respond to the invocation of the supplicant when the person calls upon Me. So let them respond to Me [by obedience] and believe in Me that they may be [rightly] guided (Baqarah: 186) [1].

هُنَالِكَ دَعَا زَكَرِيَّا رَبَّهُ قَالَ رَبِّ هَبْ لِي مِن لَّدُنْكَ ذُرِّيَّةً طَيِّبَةً إِنَّكَ سَمِيعُ الدُّعَاء {آل عمران/38} فَنَادَتْهُ الْمَلآئِكَةُ وَهُوَ قَائِمٌ يُصَلِّي فِي الْمِحْرَابِ أَنَّ اللهَ يُبَشِّرُكَ بِيَحْيَى مُصَدِّقًا بِكَلِمَةٍ مِّنَ اللهِ وَسَيِّدًا وَحَصُورًا وَنَبِيًّا مِّنَ الصَّالِحِينَ {آل عمران/39}

At that, Zechariah called upon his Lord, saying, "My Lord, grant me from Yourself a good offspring. Indeed, You are the Hearer of supplication." So the angels called him while he was standing in prayer in the sanctuary, "Indeed, Allah gives you good tidings of John the Baptist, confirming a word from Allah and [who will be] honorable, and utterly chaste, and a prophet from among the righteous. (Al-Imran: 38-39) [1].

SELECTED PRAYERS OF THE PROPHET ﷺ — DUAS OF RASULULLAH ﷺ

Peace and Blessings on the Prophet ﷺ —Salawat

1. اَللَّهُمَّ صَلِّ عَلٰى سَيِّدِنَا مُحَمَّدٍ وعَلٰي الِ سَيِّدِنَا مُحَمَّدٍ كَمَا صَلَّيْتَ عَلٰى سَيِّدِنَا إِبْرٰهِيمَ
وعَلٰي الِ سَيِّدِنَا إِبْرٰهِيمَ إِنَّكَ حَمِيدٌ مَجِيدٌ[14]

   O Allah! Send Your blessings upon our beloved Prophet, teacher, and role model Muhammad and the family of our beloved Prophet, teacher, and role model Muhammad as You sent blessings upon our role model Abraham and the family of our beloved Prophet, teacher, and role model Abraham. Truly You are the Owner of Praise, the Glorious [3].

   إِنَّ هَذِهِ أُمَّتُكُمْ أُمَّةً وَاحِدَةً وَأَنَا رَبُّكُمْ فَاعْبُدُونِ {الأنبياء/92}[15]

   VERILY, [O you who believe in Me,] this community of yours is one single community, since I am the Sustainer of you all: worship, then, Me [alone]!" (Anbiya:92) [2]

   وَإِنَّ هَذِهِ أُمَّتُكُمْ أُمَّةً وَاحِدَةً وَأَنَا رَبُّكُمْ فَاتَّقُونِ {المؤمنون/52}[16]

   And, verily, this community of yours is one single community, since I am the Sustainer of you all: remain, then, conscious of Me!" [2] (Mu'minun:52)

---

14. Allahumma salli ala sayyidina Muhammad wa ala ali sayyidina Muhammad kama sallayta ala sayyidina Ibrahim wa ala ali sayyidina Ibrahim innaka Hamidun Majid.
15. Inna haaziheee ummatukum ummatanw waahidatanw wa Ana Rabbukum fa'budoon.
16. Wa inna haaziheee ummatukum ummatanw waahidatanw wa Ana Rabbukum fattaqoon.

الْيَوْمَ أَكْمَلْتُ لَكُمْ دِينَكُمْ وَأَتْمَمْتُ عَلَيْكُمْ نِعْمَتِي وَرَضِيتُ لَكُمُ الإِسْلاَمَ دِينًا فَمَنِ اضْطُرَّ فِي مَخْمَصَةٍ غَيْرَ مُتَجَانِفٍ لِّإِثْمٍ فَإِنَّ اللهَ غَفُورٌ رَّحِيمٌ {المائدة/3}[17]

This day, I have perfected for you your religion and completed My favor upon you and have approved for you Islam as religion. As for him, however, who is driven [to what is forbidden] by dire necessity and not by an inclination to sinning—behold, God is much-forgiving, a dispenser of grace. (Maidah: 3) [2] [3].

It is important in religious practices to connect oneself to the authentic source. People from both the past and current days can claim different spiritual and religious experience. Yet, if it is not connected to the authentic source then, it is most likely to be waswasa (evil inclinations) of the nafs and shaytan. In this sense, salawat[18] can also be this rope of connection with the word salli to our main teacher al-Mustafa, the Chosen One, al-Habib, the Loved One, Muhammad, Rasullullah ﷺ. Yet, one can extend this connection to other chosen ones like Prophet Ibrahim[19] and other mursalin (messengers) as our main teacher Rasullullah ﷺ taught us. This connection of salawat and rope forms a circle of ummah, inna ummatukum ummatun wahidun[20] in front of Allah سبحانه وتعالى as mentioned "wa Ana Rabbukum fa'budun[21]." In this case, this religious practice or experience is not a personal, un-genuine, false, inauthentic or something made-up but it has the strongest roots as the religion that Rabbul A'lamin[22] is pleased

17. Alyawma akmaltu lakum deenakum wa atmamtu 'alaikum ni'matee wa radeetu lakumul Islaama deenaa; famanidturra fee makhmasatin ghaira mutajaanifil li ismin fa innallaaha Ghafoorur Raheem.
18. Expressions and phrases of blessings and peace for the Prophet Muhammad. It can be also the expressions and phrases of blessings and peace for the other Prophets of Allah such as Abraham, Moses, and Jesus.
19. Abraham
20. "This community of yours is one single community" (Anbiya:92) [2]
21. "I am the Sustainer of you all: worship, then, Me [alone]!" (Anbiya:92) [2]
22. Sustainer and Nourisher of all worlds, and universes.

with as mentioned, al yawma akmaltu lakum dinakum wa radidu bikum Islami dina.[23]

Therefore, similar to making dhikr such as subhanAllah[24], Alhamdulillah[25], or Allahu Akbar[26], salawat[27] is a dhikr too. It reminds the person to be the follower of Rasullullah ﷺ. It builds humbleness and humility that our connection with Allah سبحانه وتعالى comes truly with the teachings of Rasulullah ﷺ. and Rasulullah ﷺ was taught by Allah سبحانه وتعالى.

In some contexts, we say that yes, our connections come from Allah سبحانه وتعالى and we connect in religion directly to Allah سبحانه وتعالى. Yet, at the same time, in order not to be like Shaytan, we say that our leader and imam and connection point is Rasullullah ﷺ. Like a father, the Prophet ﷺ loves us, taught us, and worried about us. Not giving the rightful due of Rasulullah ﷺ is disobeying Allah سبحانه وتعالى. Just like disobeying one's parents is a great sin, disobeying Rasulullah ﷺ can take one out of the religion although he or she may claim that this person is a Muslim.

In this regard, salawat is a representation of this due. Again, we are the ones benefitting from this salawat and not necessarily Rasulullah ﷺ. We show our gratefulness by saying, "Oh Allah, although I have many shortcomings, but yet, I am the follower of

23. "This day I have perfected for you your religion and completed My favor upon you and have approved for you Islam as religion." (Maidah: 3) [2] [3].
24. All the perfection and glory truly belongs to Allah and fully credited to Allah. Allah is far beyond from all the negative, wrong, and imperfect constructions, imaginations, and thoughts of people.
25. All gratitude, thanks, appreciation truly belongs to Allah and fully credited to Allah.
26. Allah is always Greater, and the Most High. Allah is beyond and above all your implicit and explicit deities, fears, attachments, and shelters.
27. Expressions and phrases of blessings and peace for the Prophet Muhammad. It can also be the expressions and phrases of blessings and peace for the other Prophets of Allah such as Abraham, Moses, and Jesus.

Rasulullah ﷺ whom You sent us. Please forgive me for the sake of my connection with him ﷺ through the salawat."

When the person genuinely has this concern, they may experience the benefits of salawat in this life. There are numerous incidents reported where Rasulullah ﷺ comes to help a person in dreams and in different means even in this world. Yet, it is expected, and inshAllah hoped that his biggest help ﷺ will be after death when the person is in most need during the accountability in front of Allah سبحانه وتعالى.

Prayer—Dhikr

2. سُبْحَانَ اللهِ وَبِحَمْدِهِ[28]

Abu Huraira (Ra) narrated that the Prophet ﷺ said: "Whoever recites 100 times Glory and praise is to Allah—subhanAllah wa bihamdihi—in the morning and at night, no one can reach the level of the reward of this person on the Day of Judgment except a person who said similar or more than this person [4].

The two critical phrases in the above narration is tanzih[29] and tasbih[30] with SubhanAllah[31], and Hamd[32] with Alhamdullillah[33]. One can ask why these two phrases are critical. SubhanAllah removes everything in one's mind and heart about any wrong and negative teachings about Allah سبحانه وتعالى. This can be called tanzih in its technical term. Then, it directs the person to the correct understanding of tawhid. The second phrase is hamd which is the disposition of always having gratitude to Allah سبحانه وتعالى but not being ungrateful and unthankful in all life's dispositions. One can see that in the below ayah as:

28. SubhanAllahi wa bihamdihi.
29. Negation. In terminological meaning, they are ideas, thoughts and constructions about what Allah سبحانه وتعالى is Not.
30. Same root word with Subhan, remembering Allah سبحانه وتعالى, making dhikr, and glorfying Allah سبحانه وتعالى.
31. All the perfection and glory belongs to Allah. Allah is far beyond from all the negative, wrong, and imperfect constructions, imaginations, and thoughts of people.
32. Gratitude and appreciation. Gratitude and appreciation. This word is unique, only used for Allah to express gratitude, thankfulness and appreciation.
33. Hamd is for Allah.

بِسْمِ اللهِ الرَّحْمَنِ الرَّحِيمِ

إِذَا جَاءَ نَصْرُ اللَّهِ وَالْفَتْحُ {النصر/1} وَرَأَيْتَ النَّاسَ يَدْخُلُونَ فِي دِينِ اللَّهِ أَفْوَاجًا {النصر/2} فَسَبِّحْ بِحَمْدِ رَبِّكَ وَاسْتَغْفِرْهُ إِنَّهُ كَانَ تَوَّابًا {النصر/3}

When the victory of Allah has come and the conquest. And you see the people entering into the religion of Allah in multitudes. Then exalt [Him] with praise of your Lord and ask forgiveness of Him. Indeed, He is ever Accepting of repentance. (An-Nasr: 1–3) [1]

The wording that is used is فَسَبِّحْ بِحَمْدِ رَبِّكَ[34]. The teaching of this ayah is projected in the teaching of the Prophet ﷺ as SubhanAllahi wa bihamdihi. As the Prophet ﷺ teaches us how to implement the Quran, one can clearly see this perspective in the above narration, Allahu A'lam[35]. It is common to witness that Rasulullah ﷺ embodied all the teachings of Quran. Therefore, when it was asked to his wife about the character of Rasulullah ﷺ, the answer was very beautifully and briefly expressed as "Rasulullah ﷺ was the walking Quran" [4]. In our terms, if the Quran is the Book, Rasulullah ﷺ was the workbook to show us the practice and application of the Book.

34. Then exalt [Him] with praise of your Lord. (An-Nasr: 1–3) [1]
35. Allah knows the best.

3. اللَّهُمَّ أَنْتَ السَّلَامُ وَمِنْكَ السَّلَامُ تَبَارَكْتَ وَتَعَالَيْتَ يَا ذَا الْجَلَالِ وَالْإِكْرَامِ[36]

O Allah! You are the Source of Peace, and all peace comes from You. Blessed are You and Exalted, Possessor of Majesty and Bounty! [4].

One of the names of Allah is As-Salam. In Surah[37] Yasin, there is the word salam[38] as سَلَامٌ قَوْلًا مِن رَّبٍّ رَّحِيمٍ[39], (Yasin: 58). Some of the scholars mention that Yasin is the heart of the Quran as mentioned by the Prophet ﷺ [5] because salam, peace and tranquility, come from Rabbul Alamin. In this perspective all the sources of tranquility, peace and calmness are in the meanings of salam. Therefore, as soon as the person finishes the prayer, the person asks immediately from Allah سبحانه وتعالى an immediate treat or fruit saying "Oh Allah, please send upon me calmness, tranquility and peace."

When the person is constantly worried about other things, this dua is very critical to repeat after each prayer and especially when and if the person is in distress.

One can also view that the immediate fruit of the salah[40] is peace and tranquility in the person's heart and mind. There is an even greater reward later from Allah سبحانه وتعالى. When the Prophet ﷺ mentions there are two rewards for the fasting person, with one being at the time of breaking the fast and a bigger reward later given by Allah سبحانه وتعالى after death [3] [4]. Similarly, after finishing each salah the immediate reward, fruit or pleasure is the sakina and tranquility in the heart and mind detaching oneself from the fears, anxieties and stresses. Therefore, in the Quran, in many

36. Allahumma antas salam wa minkas salam tabarakta wa ta'alayta ya dhal jalali wal ikram.
37. Chapter.
38. Peace.
39. [And], Peace," a word from a Merciful Lord [1].
40. Five-times daily prayers.

places, for the stresses, fears and anxieties that require patience, Allah سبحانه وتعالى mentions sabr[41], the practice of patience, with salah as each salah brings the stamina, calmness and tranquility to be patient, Allahu A'lam.

4. اَللَّهُمَّ أَنْتَ أَحَقُّ مَنْ ذُكِرَ وَأَحَقُّ مَنْ عُبِدَ وَأَنْصَرُ مَنِ ابْتُغِيَ وَأَرْأَفُ مَنْ مَلَكَ وَأَجْوَدُ مَنْ سُئِلَ وَأَوْسَعُ مَنْ أَعْطَى، أَنْتَ الْمَلِكُ لاَ شَرِيكَ لَكَ وَالْفَرْدُ لَا نِدَّ لَكَ كُلُّ شَيْءٍ هَالِكٌ إِلاَّ وَجْهَكَ لَنْ تُطَاعَ إِلاَّ بِإِذْنِكَ وَلَنْ تُعْصَى إِلاَّ بِعِلْمِكَ. تُطَاعُ فَتَشْكُرُ وَتُعْصَى فَتَغْفِرُ، أَقْرَبُ شَهِيدٍ وَأَدْنَى حَفِيظٍ، حُلْتَ دُونَ النُّفُوسِ وَأَخَذْتَ بِالنَّوَاصِي وَكَتَبْتَ الْآثَارَ وَنَسَخْتَ الْآجَالَ[42]

O Allah! You are the most worthy of remembrance and the most worthy of worship. You are the best helper of all those who are sought [for help], the most compassionate of owners, the most generous of those who are petitioned, and the most liberal of those who give. You are the Sovereign without associate, You are the only being without any equal or associate. Everything perishes except You. You are not obeyed except by Your leave and You are not disobeyed except in Your knowledge. When You are obeyed You reward in return, and when You are disobeyed You are forgiving. You are the closest Witness and the nearest Protector. You block [desires of] selves, and You grasp them by the neck. You have recorded their actions and set down their last moments [6].

---

41. Patience.
42. Allahumma anta ahaqqu ma zukira, wa ahaqqu man u'bida, wa ansaru manibtigha, wa arafu man malaka, wa ajwada ma suila, wa awsa'u man a'ta, Anta Maliku la sharika lak, walfardu nidda laka, Kulli Shayin halikun illa wajhak, Lan tuta' illahi iznik wa lan tu'sa illa bi'lmik, Tuta' Fatashkuru, Tu'sa fatagfiru, aqrabu shahidin, wa anta hafizin, hulta duna annufus wa akhazta binnawasi, wa katabta alathara, nasakhta ajal.

This dua is very critical in terms of having some realization of who Allah سبحانه وتعالى is. The person can remember others, the loved ones, the family members, places, memories etc. As this dua mentions from all the ones remembered, the best, the worthiest, and the most rewarding is remembering Allah سبحانه وتعالى as mentioned with the expression 'Allahumma anta ahaqqu ma zukira[43]'. What is the reason for this? Because of the following points:

- Anta Maliku la sharika lak: all the ownerships, authorities are temporary except Yours, Ya Allah!
- La fardu nidda laka: there is nothing equal to You, Oh Allah!
- Kulli Shayin halikun illa wajhak: everything that I remember from my loved ones and all the memories are going to die, terminate except You, Ya Allah!
- Lan tuta' illa biznik wa lan tu'sa illa bi'lmik: Nothing happens, even worship or rebellious acts, without Your allowance and knowledge Oh Allah!

After all this, Who is Allah سبحانه وتعالى ? Allah سبحانه وتعالى is the One:

- Tuta' Fatashkuru: Who accepts the worship of the creation and is pleased about it
- Tu'sa fatagfiru: Who forgives and accepts repentance although there are disrespectful behaviors to You, Ya Allah!

The expression 'Allahumma anta ahaqqu ma zukira' is key because during the day, there are a lot of things that require attention. They are all considered distractions compared to remembering Allah سبحانه وتعالى. In this perspective, a person can find the true tranquility/sakina, comfort and peace in the remembrance of Allah سبحانه وتعالى in this dunya, after death in the qabir and in the afterlife.

43. *O Allah! You are the most worthy of remembrance.*

The expression 'Allahumma anta ahaqqu ma zukira' reminds the person that when the person is in the darkness of not having embodiment of the iman, this dua is another means to remind the person who is the most worthy, most deserving to be engaged with, and who is the one who deserves to be turned to.

The value of this dua is especially shown when someone is lonely and no one is around him or her. Or, the person does not want to interact with any human but he or she wants to turn to Allah سبحانه وتعالى. When the person reads this dua at this spiritual state, then this dua can have a special effect on the person inshAllah.

5. لَا إِلَهَ إِلَّا اللهُ وَحْدَهُ لَا شَرِيكَ لَهُ، لَهُ الْمُلْكُ ولَهُ الْحَمْدُ يُحْيِي وَيُمِيتُ وَهُوَ حَيٌّ لَا يَمُوتُ بِيَدِهِ الْخَيْرُ وَهُوَ عَلَى كُلِّ شَيْءٍ قَدِيرٌ[44]

There is no god but Allah, alone without associate. Allah's is the dominion, and all praise and appreciation is to Allah. Allah gives life and brings death, but Allah is the All-Living who never dies. All goodness is in Allah's hands, and Allah has power over all things [5].

The expression 'La ilaha illa Allah's wahdahu La sharika lahu'[45] can indicate that it is important to remember Allah سبحانه وتعالى with pure tawhid and renew the iman repetitively. When one has a covenant with Allah سبحانه وتعالى then they try to act accordingly at all times including the possibly difficult times and places such as in a market place in order not to break this covenant regarding ethics and morality. Ultimately, this affects one's firm iman in Allah سبحانه وتعالى.

The expression 'Lahul Mulku wa lahul Hamdu, Yuhyi Wa Yumit[46]' can suggest that in reality, all thanks and gratitude belongs to Allah سبحانه وتعالى, especially when one sees different bounties in a market place. Hence, one should be not arrogant with their purchase, wealth and money but remember that Allah سبحانه وتعالى can make the person die at any time and replace the person with another virtuous a'bd[47].

44. La ilaha illa Allahu wahdahu La sharika lahu. Lahul Mulku wa lahul Hamdu, Yuhyi Wa Yumit. Wa Huwa Hayyun la Yamut, biyedihil khayru, wa Huwa a'la kulli shayin Qadir.
45. There is no god but Allah, alone without associate.
46. His is the dominion, and all praise is to Him. He gives life and brings death.
47. The true lover and therefore worshipper, bowing with love, respect, and gratitude for Allah.

In this perspective, the expression 'Wa Huwa Hayyun la Yamut, biyedihil khayru, wa Huwa a'la kulli shayin Qadir[48]' can allude that the only One who does not die and is always Alive and Watching is Allah سبحانه وتعالى. Therefore, if the person wants something good in all engagements including buying, selling or any new venture, the person should know that the source of all good is from Allah سبحانه وتعالى, all good is owned by Allah سبحانه وتعالى. Therefore, the person should ask all the good in this dua including all the mental and emotional discourses from Allah سبحانه وتعالى before they engage themselves physically in an action. Because, Allah سبحانه وتعالى can do anything for the person, Allah سبحانه وتعالى is all Powerful.

A person can spend all his energy on doing good. But, if he does not understand 'biyadihil khayr[49]', then he could be wasting all his energy and only falling into a state of misery. Therefore, begging Allah سبحانه وتعالى constantly can open the doors of khayr (goodness) and it is the key to open the door of khayr. When sometimes a person is mislead by a chain of khayrs, and at one point, he can now try to do the next khayr by forgetting this truth then, this can be the point he loses and can become worse than shaytan.

Sometimes, our habits instill an empowerment of the self although we have no ability to establish the concept of self-sufficiency, and in reality this signals a very secret arrogance. Yet, if the person is in the list of good people (abrar), Allah سبحانه وتعالى can at any point switch off the button of khayr, and the person can be taken out from this list and be in useless self-struggles and misery in self destruction of themselves with their energy. May Allah سبحانه وتعالى protect me and all of us. Amen.

---

48. But He is the All-Living who never dies. All goodness is in His hands, and He has power over all things.
49. All goodness is in His hands,

6. اَللّٰهُمَّ بَارِكْ لَنَا فِى رَجَبَ وَ شَعْبَانَ وَ بَلِّغْنَا رَمَضَانَ[50]

O Allah! Make the months of Rajab and Sha'ban blessed for us, and let us reach the month of Ramadan [6].

It is important to recognize the ni'mahs (blessings) of Allah سبحانه وتعالى and that Allah سبحانه وتعالى is the Real Giver. When we enjoy our time in worship and prayer, then this is a ni'mah from Allah سبحانه وتعالى. In this regard, the month spans of Rajab, Sha'ban or Ramadan are also a means of enjoying our time with Allah سبحانه وتعالى. If Allah سبحانه وتعالى makes the connection, prayers, and 'ibadah[51] more rewarding and easier for us, we should thank Allah سبحانه وتعالى by first recognizing all the ayyamullah[52]. With this recognition, we ask Allah سبحانه وتعالى that Allah سبحانه وتعالى does not deprive us from these extra bonus times in these three months as mentioned with this dua. Although for some of the awliya[53], every day is one of those days, and every second is a time in laylatul qadr[54]. Yet, for the heedless ones like us, these duas put us in perspective of the importance of time, Allahu A'lam.

7. اَللّٰهُمَّ اغْفِرْ لِي وَاهْدِنِي وَارْزُقْنِي وَعَافِنِي (١٠)[55]

O Allah! Forgive me, guide me, provide for me, and keep me healthy, (repeating ten times) [4].

The time of tahajjud[56] is where the duas are accepted by Allah سبحانه وتعالى. This dua is a key dua which has the condensed form of what one can ask from Allah سبحانه وتعالى in short and precise wording at any time and especially at the times of praying tahajjud. Tahajjud is a time that one can ask with persistence, begging and crying. Therefore, 10 times repetition is important to show this embodiment of insistence and begging to Allah سبحانه وتعالى.

50. Allahumma Bariklana fi Rajaba wa shabana wa ballighna Ramadan.
51. Worship.
52. The days of Allah سبحانه وتعالى.
53. The ones close to Allah سبحانه وتعالى.
54. Night of qadr, night of power.
55. Allahumma aghfirlii wahdini warzuqni wa a'fini.
56. Night Prayers.

8. رَبَّنَا آتِنَا فِي الدُّنْيَا حَسَنَةً وَفِي الْآخِرَةِ حَسَنَةً وَقِنَا عَذَابَ النَّارِ بِرَحْمَتِكَ يَا أَرْحَمَ الرَّاحِمِينَ[57]

"Our Lord! Grant us goodness in this life and in the Hereafter, and save us from the torment of the Hellfire," [1] (Baqara 2:201) *through Your mercy, O Most Merciful of the Merciful!* [3]

This dua is a general dua to remind the person to always ask for the good from Allah سبحانه وتعالى and to ask for protection from the evil and bad both in this dunya[58] and akhirah[59].

Constantly asking for good to come during the encounters of the day, the minute or the second is very important. The person does not know what evil may happen at any time. Therefore, realizing this in each prayer in tashahud[60] and asking from Allah سبحانه وتعالى can stop the evils from coming and reaching the person.

As the expression 'bi rahmatika ya arhamurrahimin[61]' is attached to this dua, it can also be attached to any dua. This expression is a key reminder for the person that receiving of all the good, and protection against evil is from the Rahmah[62] of Allah سبحانه وتعالى.

---

57. Rabbana Atina fidunya hasanatan wa fil akhirati hasanatan wa qina a'zaba annar, bi rahmatika ya arhamarrahimin!
58. Life in this world.
59. Life in the afterlife.
60. The sitting position in the prayer.
61. Through Your mercy, O Most Merciful of the Merciful.
62. Mercy and Grace.

Morning and Evening Prayers—Sabah/Masah

9. اَلْحَمْدُ للهِ الَّذِيَ أَحْيَانَا بَعْدَ مَا أَمَاتَنَا وَإِلَيْهِ النُّشُورُ لَا إِلَهَ إِلَّا أَنْتَ سُبْحَانَكَ اللَّهُمَّ
أَسْتَغْفِرُكَ لِذَنْبِي وَأَسْأَلُكَ رَحْمَتَكَ[63]

Praise be to Allah who has revived us after death, and unto Allah is the Resurrection. There is no god but You, Glorified are You, O Allah! I seek Your forgiveness for my sins, and I ask You for Your mercy [3].

After the person wakes up, there are steps to follow. They are hamd, tahlil, istigfar, knowledge, and istikamah[64], guidance.

One can see that the purpose of the creation according to some scholars besides worship, 'ubudiyyah[65] to Allah سبحانه وتعالى, is to learn and increase one's knowledge in one's relationship with Allah سبحانه وتعالى. According to some scholars [7], the expression li ya'budun means li ya'rifun (51:56) which means, "We created humans and jinn to learn and increase one's knowledge in one's relationship with Allah instead of the widely accepted and translated meaning that, "We created the humans and jinn to worship[66]".

63. Alhamdulillahi allazi ahyana ba'da ma matana wa ilayhi annushur. La ilaha illa Anta. Subhanaka. Allahumma astagfiruka lizanbi, wa asaluka rahmataka.
64. Following the Divine Guidance incessantly and continuously.
65. One's true relationship with Allah as the Creator and creation through appreciation, dedication, and worship.
66. Surah Zariyat:56.

10. اللَّهُمَّ بِكَ أَصْبَحْنَا وَبِكَ أَمْسَيْنَا وَبِكَ نَحْيَا وَبِكَ نَمُوتُ وَإِلَيْكَ النُّشُورُ[67]

Oh Allah!, we reached the morning with Your Grace and Mercy, we reached the night with Your Grace and Mercy, we become alive with Your Order and Permission, we die with Your Order and Permission, and we will return to You.

Abu Hurairah (Ra) narrated from the Prophet ﷺ that when the Prophet ﷺ reached the morning/night time, he used to say the above dua [8](5068), [9](3868), [10](2/354).

It is important to understand when the person really wakes up after sleep it is with the Fadl and Rahmah [68]of Allah سبحانه وتعالى. We can take some of the things in life for granted, such as the cycles of sleeping and waking up accompanied with the changes of the day and night. These are some of the habitual things that happen out of our control and we may take them for granted. In these instances, it is important to ask and have empathy with the people who cannot sleep who have insomnia with sleep disorders or, the people who are always in the state of being asleep. Another scenario can be for the people who live close to the northern or southern poles, where they have limited sunlight or limited darkness. They can perhaps better embody the above prayer of the Prophet ﷺ because they don't take these cycles for granted because in these locations, this change is not a daily cycle for them.

67. Allahumma bika asbahna wa bika amsayna wa bika nahya wa bika namuutu wa ilayka annushoor.
68. Grace and Mercy.

The other expressions 'bika nahya[69]' and 'bika namut[70]' is the proclamation of people's lives and deaths that they all depend on Allah سبحانه وتعالى. Something that may seem random could happen and cause a person to die. Or something that may seem random could happen and cause a person to be sick. What we see as random in its essence is all and fully under the control of Allah سبحانه وتعالى. Therefore, the preposition 'ba', ب, with, is critical that even some of the scholars embedded huge meanings in this word. The Quran starts with this preposition 'ba' as bismillahi Rahmani Rahim. This alludes again to a similar meaning that the person constantly should remember in all life affairs that one is always dependent on Allah سبحانه وتعالى.

69. *We become alive with Your Order and Permission.*
70. We die with Your Order and Permission.

11. أَصْبَحْنَا وَأَصْبَحَ الْمُلْكُ لله لاَ شَرِيكَ لَهُ لاَ إِلٰهَ إِلاَّ هُوَ وَإِلَيْهِ النُّشُورُ، اَللَّهُمَّ فَاطِرَ السَّمٰوَاتِ وَالْأَرْضِ عَالِمَ الْغَيْبِ وَالشَّهَادَةِ رَبَّ كُلِّ شَيْءٍ وَمَلِيكَهُ أَشْهَدُ أَنْ لاَ إِلٰهَ إِلاَّ أَنْتَ أَعُوذُ بِكَ مِنْ شَرِّ نَفْسِي وَشَرِّ الشَّيْطَانِ وَشَرَكِهِ وَأَنْ أَقْتَرِفَ عَلٰى نَفْسِي سُوءًا أَوْ أَنْ أَجُرَّهُ عَلٰى مُسْلِمٍ (٤)[71]

The morning has broken upon us and upon the creation, and all belongs to Allah. He is without associate, there is no god but Him, and unto Him is the resurrection. O Allah, Creator of the heavens and earth in a certain system, Knower of the unseen and the manifest, and Lord and Owner of everything! I bear witness that there is no god but You. I seek refuge in You from the evil of myself, the evil of Satan and his traps, and from committing wrong to myself or another Muslim [8].

One of the key words in this dua is mulk[72]. Allah سبحانه وتعالى has the mulk, "Tabaraka allazi biyadihil mulk, wa huwa ala kulli shayin qadiir,[73]" as mentioned in the Quran (al-Mulk:1).

No one has the right to say, "Why is it like this or why is it not like this?" for every occurrence. But, knowing Allah سبحانه وتعالى with all the other attributes and names such as Ar-Rahim, Ar-Rahman, Ar-Rauf, Al-Karim, As-Salam, and all the others, Allah سبحانه وتعالى is so kind that all the incidents come with softness, care, kindness, with hikmah, wisdom and purpose. Therefore, one should make hamd to Allah سبحانه وتعالى for that as mentioned يُسَبِّحُ لِله مَا فِي السَّمَاوَاتِ وَمَا فِي الْأَرْضِ لَهُ الْمُلْكُ وَلَهُ الْحَمْدُ وَهُوَ عَلَى كُلِّ شَيْءٍ قَدِير[74] التغابن/1}

71. Asbahna wa asbaha almulku lillah. La sharika lahu. La ilaha ill ahu, wa ilayhi annushur. Allahumma fatirata assamawati walardi a'limal ghaybi washadati rabba kulli shayin wa malikahu. Ashadu an la ilaha illa anta. A'uzu bika min sharri nafsi, wa sharri ashaytan, sharakihi, wa an aqtarifa 'ala nafsi suuan aw an ajurrahu a'la Muslim.

72. Dominion

73. *Blessed is He in whose hand is dominion, and He is over all things competent.*

74. Tabaraka allazi lahu mulk wala hul hamd.

"Whatever is in the heavens and whatever is on the earth is exalting Allah. To Him belongs dominion, and to Him belongs [all] praise, and He is over all things competent" [1]

For example, it is said that driving is a privilege but not a right. Similarly, being a creation of Allah سبحانه وتعالى and existing is a privilege but not a right, Allahu A'lam.

12. أَصْبَحْنَا عَلٰى فِطْرَةِ الْإِسْلَامِ وَكَلِمَةِ الْإِخْلَاصِ وَعَلٰى دِينِ نَبِيِّنَا مُحَمَّدٍ وَعَلٰى مِلَّةِ أَبِينَآ إِبْرٰهِيمَ حَنِيفاً مُسْلِماً وَمَا كَانَ مِنَ الْمُشْرِكِينَ[75]

We have risen with the pristine way of Islam, with the testimony of sincerity, as a member of the nation of our forefather Abraham the pure Muslim who was not among the polytheists, who turned toward the Lord, following the religion of Prophet Muhammad (peace and blessings be upon him) [11] [10].

Each change, each new day or night require renewal of one's iman, renewal of the core of tawhid and renewal of one's connection with Rasulullah ﷺ. Each time, each change and during the course of day and night, the person is constantly in different engagements. Complementary to this dua, asking from Allah سبحانه وتعالى by reciting "aslihli sha'ni kullih[76]" is also suggested by Rasulullah ﷺ can be very important.

75. Asbahna 'ala fitratil Islam, wa kalimatil ikhlas, wa a'la diini nabiyyana Muhammad, wa a'la millata abina, Ibrahim, hanifan musliman, wa ma kana min al-mushrikiin.
76. Oh Allah, rectify all my engagements and occupations

13. اَللَّهُمَّ إِنِّيَ أَصْبَحْتُ أُشْهِدُكَ وَأُشْهِدُ حَمَلَةَ عَرْشِكَ وَمَلٰئِكَتَكَ وَجَمِيعَ خَلْقِكَ بِأَنَّكَ أَنْتَ اللهُ الَّذِي لاَ إِلٰهَ إِلاَّ أَنْتَ وَأَنَّ مُحَمَّداً عَبْدُكَ وَرَسُولُكَ[77] (٣)

O Allah! Upon the breaking of this day, I do bear witness before You, before the bearers of Your Throne, Your angels, and before all of Your creation that You are Allah besides whom there is no other god and that Muhammad is Your creation, seeker, worshipper, adorer, and Messenger [8].

This dua is very important in the daily renewal of the iman that the person underlines the core of tawhid by making witness of Allah سبحانه وتعالى, the elect angels and all the creation. As one may realize, true tawhid includes fully believing and embodying the nubuwwah (prophethood) of Rasulullah ﷺ.

77. Allahumma inni asbahtu ushiduka wa ushhidu hamalata arshika wa malaaikata wa jamiia khalqika bi annaka anta Allah, Allazi La ilaha illa anta, wa anna Muhammadan a'bduka wa rasuluk.

Protection—Ta'wiz

14. أَعُوذُ بِكَلِمَاتِ اللهِ التَّامَّاتِ مِنْ شَرِّ مَا خَلَقَ[78]

> *A man came to the Prophet ﷺ and said: "Oh Messenger of God, I was stung by a scorpion yesterday night." The Prophet ﷺ said: "When it became night if you said, "I take refuge in the full, complete, comprehensive, and perfect words of God from the evil and harm of what God created", then nothing would have harmed you,"* [4] [8].

According to the above testimony of the Prophet ﷺ, it is important for a person to take a position against all the unexpected evils in life. This is mainly performed by supplication and prayers. In this case, the Prophet ﷺ shows the antidote curing words to protect oneself. This alludes to the importance of knowledge and learning in Islam in order to cope accordingly against the difficulties of life and prepare oneself for the afterlife. The above wordings of the Prophet ﷺ are widely practiced litanies among the Muslims to protect oneself against all evil renderings. The Prophet ﷺ suggests that Muslims should read this prayer at least twice a day, immediately at night and in the morning.

In this hadith, one can try to understand what this dua means: "I take refuge in the full, complete, comprehensive, and perfect words of Allah سبحانه وتعالى from the evils and harms of what Allah سبحانه وتعالى created." As the person is weak, and there are seen and unseen evil beings, it is impossible to protect oneself physically and spiritually from all these evils and harms. When the person understands this weakness with humbleness and humility in their mind and heart, then they can take an immediate refuge in Allah سبحانه وتعالى for protection. The practical way of taking refuge in Allah سبحانه وتعالى is by verbalizing the disposition of heart and

---

78. A'uzu bikalimatillahi attaamati min sharri ma khalaq

mind that the person submits oneself to Allah سبحانه وتعالى, the Creator of everything.

The best way to verbalize it is to embody these meanings of refuge, submission and humility for Allah سبحانه وتعالى as taught to us by Allah سبحانه وتعالى in the Quran and through the teachings of the Prophet ﷺ. With all these perspectives, if one reviews the inclusivity, perfectness and completeness of this dua as, "I take refuge in the full, complete, comprehensive, and perfect words of Allah سبحانه وتعالى from the evil and harm of what Allah سبحانه وتعالى created," then this person becomes untouchable and protected from all evils and harms. Here, the disposition of the heart and mind with full submission to Allah سبحانه وتعالى is the key. If the person prays with these prophetic expressions even in a partially focused-state of heart and mind, then these words still have a protective effect on the person, Allahu A'lam.

15. أَعُوذُ بِاللهِ مِنَ الشَّيْطَانِ الرَّجِيمِ[79]

I seek refuge in Allah from Satan the accursed [4].

When the person becomes angry, the Prophet ﷺ advises the above phrase. It is important to remember to implement what the Prophet ﷺ teaches us in their apparent forms. In other words, one can just say the above phrase especially when one becomes angry. Then, there is a calming effect on the person. To increase the effect of the above phrase and others, the person should take the means of educating oneself and embody the meanings in oneself.

In other words, it is important to understand that the person is weak, and that there are seen and unseen evil beings, it is impossible to protect oneself physically and spiritually from all these evils and harms. When the person understands this weakness with humbleness and humility in their mind and heart, then they can take an immediate refuge in Allah سبحانه وتعالى for protection.

As the person feels this weakness on him or herself and makes tawakkul[80] to Allah سبحانه وتعالى then, the effect of this phrase and others can increase and prevent the person from the harm of others inshAllah.

79. A'uzu billahi min as-shaytani rajim
80. Reliance and Trust in Allah

16. اَللَّهُمَّ إِنِّي أَعُوذُ بِرِضَاكَ مِنْ سَخَطِكَ وَبِمُعَافَاتِكَ مِنْ عُقُوبَتِكَ وَأَعُوذُ بِكَ مِنْكَ، لَا أُحْصِي ثَنَاءً عَلَيْكَ أَنْتَ كَمَا أَثْنَيْتَ عَلَى نَفْسِكَ[81]

O Allah, truly I seek refuge in Your good pleasure from Your anger, in Your exemption from Your punishment, and I seek refuge in You from You. I admit that I am unable to praise You as You have praised Yourself. [4]

Allah سبحانه وتعالى mentions in this hadith that the Pleasure of Allah سبحانه وتعالى is the greatest achievement that one can reach in this life and next. In this life, if a person is engaged with the disliked engagements set by Allah سبحانه وتعالى then this may have Sakhat (displeasure) of Allah سبحانه وتعالى. In this perspective, a person can receive either Sakhat or Pleasure of Allah سبحانه وتعالى due to the different engagements throughout their day. This dua of the Prophet ﷺ teaches us to ask Allah سبحانه وتعالى for the engagements which please Allah سبحانه وتعالى during the course of the day.

The rest of this dua shows the outcomes of Pleasure and Sakhat of Allah سبحانه وتعالى in this dunya[82]. In this perspective, if someone can gain the Pleasure of Allah سبحانه وتعالى then, inshallah the afiyah[83] is given to this person by Allah سبحانه وتعالى. If the person has the Sakhat of Allah سبحانه وتعالى then the u'qubah (punishment) can be given to this person, May Allah سبحانه وتعالى protect us from this, Amin.

81. Allahumma inni a'oodhubi ridaaka min sakhatik wa bi mu'aafatika min 'uqoobatik wa a'oodhubi bika minka la uhsi thanaaun alayk anta kama athnayta 'ala nafsik.

82. World, or worldly life

83. Spiritual and bodily well-being

17. اَللَّهُمَّ لَكَ الْحَمْدُ أَنْتَ كَسَوْتَنِيهِ أَسْأَلُكَ خَيْرَهُ وَخَيْرَ مَاصُنِعَ لَهُ[84]

O Allah! To You is due all praise for You dressed me in it. I ask You for good in it and the good it was made for [8].

As all the duas of the Prophet ﷺ has its proper usage with its first meanings, they may also have some inner meanings, Allahu A'lam. In this case, when a person goes to a change in his or her body through age, surgery due to illness and others, one can possibly recite this dua as well, because the body is like a dress of the soul. Similarly, if a person goes through a habitual change in his or her life, one can also recite this dua to ask the khayr of it and protection from the evil of it. The habits are also considered as our dress that we constantly dress ourselves such as the daily awrad[85], Allahu A'lam.

18. أَعُوذُ بِاللهِ مِنَ الشَّيْطَانِ الرَّجِيمِ وَمِنْ فِتْنَتِهِ. اٰمَنْتُ بِاللهِ وَرُسُلِهِ اَللهُ أَحَدٌ، اَللهُ الصَّمَدُ، لَمْ يَلِدْ وَلَمْ يُولَدْ، وَلَمْ يَكُنْ لَهُ كُفُواً أَحَدٌ.[86] ثم يتفل عن يساره ثلا ثا

I seek refuge in Allah from Satan the accursed and from his temptations. I believe in Allah and His messengers, "Say: Allah, the One and Only! Allah, the Absolute, Eternal; He begets not, nor is He begotten. And there is none like unto Him." (Ikhlas 112)[4] (blow on the left side three times)

It is important to focus at the times of waswasa to collect oneself. The best way to focus is to seek refuge in Allah سبحانه وتعالى as mentioned fully in the meanings of Surah Ikhlas. When a person understands and embodies the Oneness, the Uniqueness and other attributes of Allah سبحانه وتعالى, then that necessitates having ikhlas[87], and one can remove the distractions and waswasa inshaAllah

---

84. Allahumma lakal hamdu anta kasawtanihi. Asaluka khayrahu wa khayra ma sunia lahu. Wa au'zu bika min sharrihi wa sharri ma sunia' lahu.

85. Plural form of wird, means daily regular and habitual spiritual engagements.

86. A'zu billahi min asshaytani rajim wa min fitnati Amantu billahi wa rusulihi, Allahu Ahad, Allahu Assamad, Lam yalid, wa lam yulad wa lam yakun lahu kufuwan ahad.

87. Sincerity.

19. أَعُوذُ بِاللهِ مِنَ الشَّيْطَانِ الرَّجِيمِ مِنْ هَمْزِهِ وَنَفْخِهِ، وَنَفْثِهِ[88]

I seek refuge in Allah from Satan the accursed and from his temptation, whispering and blowing, and spitting [10].

When a person is distracted with different thoughts this is called waswasa, or distraction of thoughts. This is against the notion of focus of the dhikr that comes with 'La ilaha illa Allah[89]'. One can realize that this can be driven either by shaytan or nafs. The waswasa can sometimes lead to anger and displeasing states of the heart and mind. In this case, the people may not want to be around this person. May Allah سبحانه وتعالى protect us.

20. أَعُوذُ بِكَلِمَاتِ اللهِ التَّامَّةِ مِنْ كُلِّ شَيْطَانٍ وَهَامَّةٍ وَمِنْ كُلِّ عَيْنٍ لَامَّةٍ[90]

I take refuge in the perfect words of Allah, from all devils and harmful animals, and from every evil eye [3].

Children can be a blessing. Especially, one may realize this when others may not have children. In these cases, and others, it is important to make shukr to Allah سبحانه وتعالى and ask the production of these children from evil eye and other harms. It is important to make dua to Allah سبحانه وتعالى as Prophet Ibrahim did to make the children be a source of piety and a means to achieve the pleasure of Allah سبحانه وتعالى as mentioned وَالَّذِينَ يَقُولُونَ رَبَّنَا هَبْ لَنَا مِنْ أَزْوَاجِنَا وَذُرِّيَّاتِنَا قُرَّةَ أَعْيُنٍ وَاجْعَلْنَا لِلْمُتَّقِينَ إِمَامًا {الفرقان/٧٤}.[91]

---

88. A'uzu billahi min asshaytani rajim wa min hamzihi, wa nafkhihi, wa nafthihi.

89. Can be translated as "there is no deity or god except Allah." This is the creed of Islam called shahadah. Whoever believes in this, is considered Muslim even though the person may not proclaim his or her faith in public, because belief is between the individual and Allah in Islam.

90. A'uzu bi kalimatillahi taamah min kulli shaytanin wa hammah wa min kulli a'ynin lammat.

91. And those who say, "Our Lord, grant us from among our wives and offspring comfort to our eyes, and make us a leader for the righteous" (Furqan:74).

21. اَللّٰهُمَّ اشْرَحْ لِي صَدْرِي وَيَسِّرْ لِي أَمْرِي وَأَعُوذُ بِكَ مِنْ وَسَاوِسِ الصَّدْرِ وَشَتَاتِ الْأَمْرِ وَفِتْنَةِ الْقَبْرِ[92]

O Allah! Open my heart, and make my affairs easy for me! I seek refuge in You from the evil whisperings felt at the heart, from that which disrupts my affairs and from the trial of the grave [12].

Each part of this dua is very critical and one can write pages on its importance and application in one's daily life. As one can see, the speech of Rasulullah ﷺ is made up of short statements with very intensive, useful, convoluted, and deep meanings. The term 'Jawami al-Kalim[93]" is used to describe the quality of the words spoken by Rasulullah [3] ﷺ. This shows that the hadith itself is a revelation from Allah سبحانه وتعالى. So, it is not, astagfirullah, a human speaking, but it is a divine revelation to Rasulullah ﷺ at a human level as a mercy from Allah سبحانه وتعالى to us about how to implement the practical and correct application of the Quran in our lives.

Therefore, the common expressions one can hear in Jum'a Khutbahs[94] as "inna asdaqa al-hadisi kitabulllah,wa ahsanal huda, hadyi Muhammadin ﷺ [95]" [3] [4] mentioned originally by Rasulullah ﷺ. This statement is not a mere a statement but summarizing the authentic epistemology in Islam developed and transferred from one generation to another for hundreds of years. In this regards, the established methodology (usul) is:

---

92. Allahumma ashrahli sadri wa yassirli amri wa au'zu bika min wa sawisin assadri wa shatati al-amri wa fitnati alqabri.
93. Conciseness of speech. A few words with dense and convoluted means. This is a specific title given and used only for the Prophet Muhammad, Rasulullah ﷺ.
94. Friday Sermons
95. The most truthful words are the Book of Allah, the Quran. The best guidance is the guidance of Rasulullah ﷺ.

- Quran
- Hadith
- Qiyas[96] & ijma'[97]

One of the themes that are mentioned in this dua is that our hearts get confused and lose focus, as a result of this, spiritual contractions and shrinkages occur in our hearts. This can lead to the feelings of depression, anxiety, uneasiness and fear. Therefore, the first part of the dua starts with the phrase of opening of the chest as Allahumma ashrah li sadri[98].

The chest is the place where the heart resides. The person is asking Allah سبحانه وتعالى to remove these negative emotional and mental dispositions from the heart and the chest. The cause of these dispositions could be due to a sin, an action, a saying, a look, a hearing, a touch or a thought that may be displeasing to Allah سبحانه وتعالى. Or, it can be due to not properly embodying La ilaha illa Allah that things can be overpowering us. Therefore, asking Allah سبحانه وتعالى the things in our lives to be easy but not difficult is very important.

Yet, some people may be still in the positions of temptations, ill thoughts or uncomfortable feelings which can be inclusive in the meaning of the word "waswasa." Waswasa is the matter of the chest and heart but not the matter of the mind. In order words, there is no logical stance for waswasa therefore it sticks to the faculties of feelings through the heart and chest. Therefore, the phrase "the temptations of the chest" refers to wasawisul sadr[99].

96. Analogy
97. Consensus, it is the consensus of scholars as its technical term.
98. *O Allah! Open my heart!*
99. *The evil whisperings felt at the heart.*

All these complex internal struggles can cause the person to have physical and spiritual messiness, defocus, and chaos as the phrase shatatil amr[100] alludes. This can be a chaotic state for the person but only the person knows it.

Lastly, another form of chaos can happen in the grave. The person can be punished (may Allah سبحانه وتعالى protect us) by something he or she may not see as something important. Rasulullah ﷺ once mentioned about a person being punished in the grave due to having filth on them but not properly washing it and another person was being punished due to backbiting [3] [4]. May Allah سبحانه وتعالى protect us, amin.

100. *Disruption of one's affairs.*

22. اَللَّهُمَّ إِنِّي أَعُوذُ بِكَ مِنْ شَرِّ مَا يَلِجُ فِي اللَّيْلِ وَشَرِّ مَا يَلِجُ فِي النَّهَارِ وَشَرِّ مَا تَهُبُّ بِهِ الرِّيَاحُ[101]

O Allah! Truly I seek refuge in You from the evil of what enters the night, the evil of what enters the day, and from the evil that blows in the wind.

This dua indicates uncertainty of one's engagement with sharr (evil). Therefore, the dua indicates the constant spiritual state of fear and hope, uncertainty and not having safety but also the disposition of immense and unceasing need to take refuge in and rely on Allah سبحانه وتعالى. There can be a lot of tests or trials that can hit a person when the person forgets this and engages oneself with certain safety dispositions as mentioned in the Quran (A fa amina ahlul-qura…):

أَفَأَمِنَ أَهْلُ الْقُرَى أَن يَأْتِيَهُمْ بَأْسُنَا بَيَاتاً وَهُمْ نَآئِمُونَ {الأعراف/97} أَوَ أَمِنَ أَهْلُ الْقُرَى أَن يَأْتِيَهُمْ بَأْسُنَا ضُحًى وَهُمْ يَلْعَبُونَ {الأعراف/98} أَفَأَمِنُواْ مَكْرَ اللّهِ فَلاَ يَأْمَنُ مَكْرَ اللّهِ إِلاَّ الْقَوْمُ الْخَاسِرُونَ {الأعراف/99}[102]

As mentioned, the requirement is for one's heart to be constantly relying on Allah سبحانه وتعالى. A second, minute, hour, or day of ghaflah[103], state of heedlessness, can attract tests or trials. May Allah سبحانه وتعالى forgive and protect us, Amin.

---

101. Allahumma inni a'uzu bika min sharri ma yaliju fil laylli wa sharri ma yaliju fin nahaari wa sharri ma tahubbu bih arriyahu.
102. Then, did the people of the cities feel secure from Our punishment coming to them at night while they were asleep? Or did the people of the cities feel secure from Our punishment coming to them in the morning while they were at play? Then, did they feel secure from the plan of Allah? But no one feels secure from the plan of Allah except the lost people, (A'raf:97–99).
103. Spiritual heedlessness, forgetfulness, and carelessness.

23. لَا إِلَهَ إِلَا اللهُ وَحْدَهُ لَا شَرِيكَ لَهُ، لَهُ الْمُلْكُ ولَهُ الْحَمْدُ يُحْيِي وَيُمِيتُ وَهُوَ حَيٌّ لَا يَمُوتُ بِيَدِهِ الْخَيْرُ وَهُوَ عَلَى كُلِّ شَيْءٍ قَدِيرٌ. بِسْمِ اللهِ اللَّهُمَّ إِنِّي أَسْأَلُكَ خَيْرَ هٰذِهِ السُّوقِ وَخَيْرَ مَا فِيهَا وَأَعُوذُ بِكَ مِنْ شَرِّهَا وَشَرِّ مَا فِيهَا. اَللَّهُمَّ إِنِّي أَعُوذُ بِكَ أَنْ أُصِيبَ فِيهَا يَمِينًا فَاجِرَةً أَوْ صَفْقَةً خَاسِرَةً[104]

There is no god but Allah, alone without associate. His is the dominion, and all praise is to Him. He gives life and brings death, but He is the All-Living who never dies. All goodness is in His hands, and He has power over all things. In the name of Allah, O Allah, I ask of You the good of this market and the goodness within it, and I seek refuge in You from its evil and the evil within it. O Allah! Verily I seek refuge in You from any suffering at this market [that might come about because] of a false oath or a poor deal [5].

In all dispositions of the person with Allah سبحانه وتعالى, the person reminds oneself that 'biyadihi alkhayru' (all goodness is in the hands of Allah (سبحانه وتعالى). Allah سبحانه وتعالى has the ultimate, and absolute source of good and khayr. Therefore, when the person tends to think that he or she has all the abilities, still Allah سبحانه وتعالى can put the person in such a position like Karun (28:76) mentioned in the Quran[105], that the person can be humiliated and degraded. Yet, this was not seen as a possibility for this person by others. Another example is that of Firawn (Pharaoh). The feelings of security can be deadly in one's relationship with Allah سبحانه وتعالى.

104. La ilaha illa Allahu wahdahu la sharika lahu, lahul mulku, wa lahu hamdu, yuhyi wa yumitu, wa huwa hayyun la yamuutu, biyadihi alkhayru, wa huwa 'ala kulli shayin qadir. Bismillahi Allahumma inni asaluka khayra hazihi assuqi wa khayra ma fiiha wa a'uzu bika min sharriha wa sharri ma fiiha. Allahumma inni a'uzu bika an useeba fiiha yameenan faajiratan aw safqatan khaasiratan.

105. Surah Qasas:76.

In addition, the dua 'Allahumma a'uzu bika an usiba fiha yaminan fajiratan[106]' can indicate the need for honesty, truth and just disposition in any dealings of life. Sometimes, a person may very much desire for something to happen. Yet, this person, although he or she can be considered religious or pious, can oversee these fundamental teachings of Islam on being with the side of truth, honesty, and justice.

Actually, another hadith of the Prophet ﷺ indicates that always being in the right, truthful and honest disposition gives an immense strength to the person and this person can maintain happiness in life. On the other hand, a person who did not establish this core teaching, can have fears, anxieties and worries due to their unjust or dishonest engagements even it is done occasionally and even if he or she is a Muslim or pious. An occasional dishonest engagement can bother the person due to their iman. Iman necessitates honesty, purity and truth. If the person does not have true iman, then lying or partaking in dishonest engagements would not bother them.

106. O Allah! Verily I seek refuge in You from any suffering at this market [that might come about because] of a false oath.

24. اَللَّهُمَّ فَاطِرَ السَّمٰوَاتِ وَالْأَرْضِ عَالِمَ الْغَيْبِ وَالشَّهَادَةِ رَبَّ كُلِّ شَيْءٍ وَمَلِيكَهُ أَشْهَدُ أَنْ لَا إِلٰهَ إِلاَّ أَنْتَ أَعُوذُ بِكَ مِنْ شَرِّ نَفْسِي وَشَرِّ الشَّيْطَانِ وَشَرَكِهِ وَأَنْ أَقْتَرِفَ عَلٰى نَفْسِي سُوءًا أَوْ أَنْ أَجُرَّهُ عَلٰى مُسْلِمٍ[107]

The morning has broken upon us and upon the creation, and all belongs to Allah. He is without associate, there is no god but Him, and unto Him is the resurrection. O Allah, Creator of the heavens and earth in a certain system, Knower of the unseen and the manifest, and Lord and Owner of everything! I bear witness that there is no god but You. I seek refuge in You from the evil of my self, the evil of Satan and his traps, and from committing wrong to myself or another Muslim [8].

It is interesting to note the source of evil is either the person's nafs as mentioned 'sharri nafsi'[108] as an internal factor. Or the source of evil is shaytan as mentioned 'wa sharri shaytani'[109] as an external agent. It is interpreted that nafs and shaytan can collaborate or cooperate for the destruction of the person, the soul (ruh) or the heart (qalb). Yet, the nafs can change or be controlled or overpowered although the nafs has the potential of doing a lot of evil compared to Shaytan which will not change. This can be represented in Adam (peace be upon him) as the person carrying the nafs who changes and asks for forgiveness from Allah سبحانه وتعالى after making a mistake compared to Iblis being the lead shaytan who did not and will not change.

107. Allahumma fatirata assamawati walardi a'limal ghaybi washadati rabba kulla shayin wa malikahu. Ashadu an la ilaha illa anta. A'uzu bika min sharri nafsi, wa sharri ashaytan, sharakihi, wa an aqtarifa ala nafsi suuan aw an ajrahu a'la Muslim.

108. From the evil of myself.

109. From the evil of Satan.

So at the end, the person with the dynamics of the ruh (soul) and qalb (heart) should work on the betterment of the nafs together. The phrase of 'wa an aqtarifa ala nafsi'[110] can indicate this possible resent, regret and change on the side of the nafs when doing something evil compared to shaytan that does not carry those feelings of regret or remorse and finally don't change.

Yes, change can be possible after the recognition, regret, and remorse of a person for their mistakes.

110. From committing wrong to myself.

Asking Forgiveness, Cleaning Heart and Mind—Istigfar

25. اَللَّهُمَّ إِنِّي ظَلَمْتُ نَفْسِي ظُلْما كَثِيرًا وَلَا يَغْفِرُ الذُّنُوبَ إِلا أَنْتَ فَاغْفِرْ لِي مَغْفِرَةً مِنْ عِنْدِكَ وَارْحَمْنِي إِنَّكَ أَنْتَ الْغَفُورُ الرَّحِيمُ[111]

O Allah! Truly I have greatly wronged my soul, and no one forgives sins except You, so forgive me with Your forgiveness, and have mercy on me, for You are the All-Forgiving, the All-Compassionate [3].

Above is a dua suggested by the Prophet ﷺ to be recited in the position of tashahud. It is important to understand that a person is constantly in the state of darkness in relation to a possible higher state of iman that he or she can reach. In other words, not knowing and appreciating Allah سبحانه وتعالى induces darkness on the self. Therefore, the person can remove this darkness by constantly accepting his or her position first and asking forgiveness from Allah سبحانه وتعالى. In this perspective, the only true being who has the authority of accepting forgiveness and forgiving is Allah سبحانه وتعالى. The people can have the shadow of this notion as the khalifah, vicegerent of Allah سبحانه وتعالى, to represent this notion of forgiving other people. In reality, the true forgiving authority is with Allah سبحانه وتعالى. Therefore, when Allah سبحانه وتعالى forgives someone then Allah سبحانه وتعالى can inspire other humans to forgive this person, Allahu A'lam.

It is very important to focus on the notion of zulm, oppression of a person on their own self. By constantly making wrong choices that displease Allah سبحانه وتعالى, the person in reality puts him or herself in darkness and oppression. At the higher level of people in their proximity to Allah سبحانه وتعالى, they try to filter not only their actions and verbal engagements but also their thoughts and emotions in order not to fall into the category of zulm. The person will be in zulm to oneself until one dies. Therefore, accepting this

111. Allahumma inni zalamtu nafsi zulman kathiran wala yaghfirudh-dhunuba illa anta, Faghfirli maghfiratan min indika war-hamni, innaka antal Ghafur-Rahim.

and asking protection from the Fadl and Rahmah of Allah سبحانه وتعالى is the key.

The expression zulman kasiran[112] can indicate the constant engagement of the person in the displeasure of Allah سبحانه وتعالى. In other words, most of the time a Muslim can involve oneself in an engagement that he or she may not realize the seriousness of this evil for the displeasure of Allah سبحانه وتعالى. As most of the people take religion as a set of rules, there is an implicit practice of separating the religion from the practical, constant, minutely details of our engagements. In this perspective, a word, a thought, a look, a touch, a bite or a hearing can lead to the displeasure of Allah سبحانه وتعالى as a zulm. Therefore, as indicated in this expression of zulman kasiran, the person should incessantly involve oneself with dua and prayer with humbleness and humility in front of Allah سبحانه وتعالى.

The expression 'wa la yaghfiru azzunuba illa anta[113]' is a critical term to embody. Sometimes, we go around and try to find solutions for our problems. But, in reality, the only source of solution is with Allah سبحانه وتعالى. Once we embody this notion, all our problems can be solved and we can be in the state of peace and tranquility, sakina. As humans, we like to reason and give importance to the immediate encounters of causality. In reality, if one embodies the notion that Allah سبحانه وتعالى is watching and has the power to execute anything at any time then the person relieves oneself from the burden and disgust of the fake helpers.

This dua is very critical to repeat. One can be in a constant state of oppression during the day and during the night. This stance with regret will keep the person going up positively in his or her relationship with Allah سبحانه وتعالى. But, if someone comprehends him or herself as flawless and not equipped with many mistakes, then this can have the true posture of an arrogant person whether the person means it or not, or whether the person realizes it or not.

112. A lot of wrongdoings.
113. No one forgives sins except You.

26. اَللَّهُمَّ اغْفِرْ لِي مَا قَدَّمْتُ وَمَا أَخَّرْتُ وَمَا أَسْرَرْتُ وَمَا أَعْلَنْتُ وَمَا أَسْرَفْتُ وَمَا أَنْتَ أَعْلَمُ بِهِ مِنِّي، أَنْتَ الْمُقَدِّمُ وَأَنْتَ الْمُؤَخِّرُ لَا إِلٰهَ إِلَّا أَنْتَ[114]

O Allah! Forgive me for what I have done and for what I will do, for what I have concealed, and what I have declared, and what I committed excess in, and for what You know best about from me. You are the Hastener, You are the Postponer, and there is no god but You [3].

It is important to cover all the possibilities of mistakes, evils, and sins when a person asks forgiveness from Allah سبحانه وتعالى.

This perspective can make the person embody the notion of humility and humbleness in front of سبحانه وتعالى. For example, a person should constantly repent to Allah for the evil renderings as mentioned as asrartu[115]. He or she should not see himself or herself as pious because of being in constant repentance. The unknown sins or evils in the past and in the future are expressed with the expression ma qadamtu wa ma akhartu[116].

This type of comprehensive approach, where a person is including all the possibilities as mentioned in the dua of the Prophet ﷺ, can relieve the person from the burden of these acts on the heart and mind. In other words, true repentance and asking forgiveness from Allah سبحانه وتعالى can relieve the person and discharge anxieties, stresses, fears and worries.

Depending on the disposition of the person asking forgiveness from Allah سبحانه وتعالى and being careful about not performing the disliked items by Allah سبحانه وتعالى, the person can then either

114. Allahumma aghfir li ma qaddammtu wa ma akhartu wa ma asrartu wa a'lantu wa ma asraftu wa ma anta a'lamu bihi minni. Antal muqaddimu wa Antal muakhiru. La ilaha illa Anta.
115. *What I committed excess in.*
116. *What I have done and for what I will do.*

be made advanced or kept behind in one's relationship with Allah SWT, Allahu A'lam.

The expressions 'ma qadammtu wa ma akhartu[117]' can indicate that a person does something but they don't know the result of it, whether it was accepted by Allah سبحانه وتعالى. Therefore, asking forgiveness from Allah سبحانه وتعالى is important. Another key word is 'wa ma asraftu[118]'. Sometimes, we are involved with things that we consider as virtuous. As we lose the balance then this virtuous act can become a sin. For example, when a person gives advice to their children, friends or family members, if the person does not keep the etiquette of hikmah[119], then this virtuous intended act can turn into a type of repulsive act instead, may Allah سبحانه وتعالى protect us.

---

117. *What I have done and for what I will do.*
118. *What I committed excess in.*
119. Wisdom, especially all the practices of the Prophet Muhammad is referred as hikmah in its technical term.

27. اَللَّهُمَّ إِنَّكَ عَفُوٌّ تُحِبُّ العَفْوَ فَاعْفُ عَنِّي [120]

O Allah!, You are Most Forgiving, and You love forgiveness; so forgive me! [5]

This dua is critical at all times. Especially during the month of Ramadan when it is known as the month of forgiveness. Therefore, the gist of this dua emphasizes with all its words the easiness of forgiveness as mentioned by the Prophet ﷺ. That if the person is not due for forgiveness in this month, then when possibly can a person redeem forgiveness. To emphasize this point of asking for forgiveness, the Prophet ﷺ uses an opposite approach to make dua against the one who cannot use this opportunity [13]. In reality, the Prophet is not making a dua against a person but emphasizing the easiness of forgiveness from Allah سبحانه وتعالى at all times but especially during this month.

This dua is also critical at times other than Ramadan as well. If the person knows and embodies that Allah سبحانه وتعالى is always Merciful and Forgiving, then the person will always go back to Allah سبحانه وتعالى. Sometimes, depending on the waswasa of shaytan and renderings of the nafs, the person may not inclined to go back to Allah سبحانه وتعالى but try to ignore or forget his or her sins or situation. This dua reminds the person to know oneself and to go back to Allah سبحانه وتعالى at all conditions and times knowing that Allah سبحانه وتعالى loves to forgive.

120. Allahumma innaka a'fun tuhibbul 'afwa fa'fu'anni.

28. اَللّٰهُمَّ آتِ نَفْسِي تَقْوَاهَا وَزَكِّهَا أَنْتَ خَيْرُ مَنْ زَكَّاهَا أَنْتَ وَلِيُّهَا وَمَوْلٰيهَا[121]

O Allah! Bring out the piety within my soul and purify it, for You are the best one to purify it; You are its Protector and Master [3].

This dua is very critical. The person's nafs constantly indulges in one action to another and the person is generally too weak to control and monitor one's nafs. Therefore, it is very critical to ask Allah سبحانه وتعالى not to leave the nafs alone but to give taqwa[122], and tazkiya[123] to it. Ultimately, asking Allah سبحانه وتعالى to befriend and protect one's nafs is the goal. Then, these ungrounded changes in one's nafs can be under the control of the One Who is in control of everything. Allahumma ja'alna minhum.

Taqwa can have different levels. One of the signs of embodiment of taqwa can be the case when the person has an opportunity to do haram but the person does not do it due to the respect, fear and love of Allah سبحانه وتعالى. One can review the hadith about the three people stuck in a cave with a rock closing the exit way. They all make dua by using this notion of embodiment of taqwa [4] (2743).

---

121. Allahumma aati nafsi taqwaha wa zakkiha anta khayru man zakkaha anta waliyyuha wa mawlaha.

122. Constant consciousness and awareness of Allah with love and attachment.

123. The process of constant spiritual cleaning of heart, soul, and mind. This is the technical name of the lifelong struggle of a person in the practice of spiritual cleaning of heart, soul and mind until one dies.

29. اَللَّهُمَّ اغْفِرْ لِي جِدِّي وَهَزْلِي وَخَطَئِي وَعَمْدِي وَكُلُّ ذَلِكَ عِنْدِي وَلَا تَحْرِمْنِي بَرَكَةَ مَا أَعْطَيْتَنِي وَلَا تَفْتِنِّي فِيمَا أَحْرَمْتَنِي[124]

O Allah! Forgive me that which [I have done] in earnest, jokingly, unintentionally, and deliberately, for all of these are to my name. Do not deprive me of blessings in that which You have provided for me, and do not try me in that which You have kept from me!

This dua is very critical to complement the previous dua. As the person is indulging in different states of mind and heart with joy, sadness, hope, hopelessness, mistakes, decisions and different dispositions during the day, one can easily be in darkness by saying, thinking and doing something displeasing to Allah سبحانه وتعالى. This dua reminds us of our constant need of connecting to Allah سبحانه وتعالى and asking protection from these different multitude of sins. May Allah سبحانه وتعالى protect us, Amin.

124. Allahumma aghfirli jiddi wa hazli wa khatai wa 'amdi wa kullu zalika I'ndi wa la tahrimni barakata ma a'taytani wa la taftinni fima ahramtani.

30. اَللَّهُمَّ اغْفِرْ وَارْحَمْ وَاعْفُ عَمَّا تَعْلَمُ وَأَنْتَ الأَعَزُّ الأَكْرَمُ[125]

O Allah! Forgive, show mercy, and pardon what You know best about, for truly You are the All-Honored with irresistible Might, the All-Generous [6].

Allah سبحانه وتعالى knows our mistakes and renderings, both those done in secret or out in the open. It is important to embody this understanding. Then, constantly asking for magfirah (forgiveness) from Allah سبحانه وتعالى is the key. When someone is asking magfirah, it is important to ask for Rahmah from Allah سبحانه وتعالى. This can mean in our colloquial language to be easy on the other person. Rahman is one of the Names of Allah سبحانه وتعالى. By revisiting our thoughts, we remember and say, "Oh Allah, I know you are Arhamu Rahimin (the Most Merciful)." Sometimes, people forget this about Allah سبحانه وتعالى.

Then, 'wa'fu'[126] comes to override one's mistakes although Allah سبحانه وتعالى knows everything 'a'mma ta'lamu[127]. The end of dua can indicate that although Allah سبحانه وتعالى can punish the person with 'ala'zzu'[128] but still Allah سبحانه وتعالى forgives and erases one's sins with 'al akramu'[129], Allahu A'lam.

As the person is in constant disposition of doing actions that is against the pleasure of Allah سبحانه وتعالى, it is important to accept this reality and go back to Allah سبحانه وتعالى continuously and ask apology, forgiveness, and beg until the person is released from these constant imposed burdens provoked by these sins.

---

125. Allahumma aghfirli wa arham wa a'fu 'amma ta'lamu wa anta al-'Azzu wa al-Akram.
126. Pardon.
127. *What You know.*
128. *Irresistible Might.*
129. *The All-Generous.*

Sometimes, the sins come and bother the person so much as mentioned in Surah Tawbah[130], the one's conscience squeezes the person meaning the person's heart shrinks and contracts spiritually and everything and everyone becomes so unbearable for this person on the earth. This inner disposition is due to the engagements of the person that is against the pleasure of Allah سبحانه وتعالى.

The solution is easy. As our Rabb, Rabbul Alamin, is All Merciful and Ar-Rahman, and Ar-Rahim, first one should accept their mistakes, then ask help and forgiveness from Allah سبحانه وتعالى. This can reset the person's sins. Yet, if the person does not do this act of constant reconnecting to Allah سبحانه وتعالى through prayers and asking tawbah, then, this person can be in self-imposed pains that make the life torture for him or her. After this unbearable torture, the next step for this person is to negate and desire the absence of some of the core teachings of iman which can ultimately stir and disturb the core, essence and pillars of iman in one's heart and mind. Ultimately, this can lead the person to kufr. Most Muslims who are in sins and argue against the teachings of Islam are in this temperament due to this effect. May Allah سبحانه وتعالى protect us. Amin.

130. [9:118].

31. اَللَّهُمَّ اغْفِرْ وَارْحَمْ وَأَنْتَ الأَعَزُّ الأَكْرَمُ. اَللَّهُمَّ اغْفِرْ وَارْحَمْ وَاعْفُ عَمَّا تَعْلَمُ إِنَّكَ أَنْتَ الأَعَزُّ الأَكْرَمُ[131]

O Allah! Forgive, and show mercy, for truly You are the Honored with irresistible Might, the All-Generous. O Allah! Forgive, show mercy, and pardon what You know best about, for truly You are the Honored with irresistible Might, the All-Generous [6].

If we analyze the above dua around the word of a'fu[132] we can remember the same word is used in different parts of the Quran.

Allah سبحانه وتعالى mentions

[133]وَهُوَ الَّذِي يَقْبَلُ التَّوْبَةَ عَنْ عِبَادِهِ وَيَعْفُو عَنِ السَّيِّئَاتِ وَيَعْلَمُ مَا تَفْعَلُونَ {الشورى/25}

Allah سبحانه وتعالى knows everything but does not take us to account from our evils and sins neither immediately nor in the full account. Yet, the concept of pardoning, and "moving on" or not acting on it, can be very difficult for a human when the person can go back and apply retribution on the other party.

Yes, a'fw[134] can come especially when the person has the means to apply retribution.

131. Allahumma aghfir warham wa anta Al-A'zzu Al-Akram. Allahumma aghfir warham wa'fu 'amman ta'lamu innaka anta Al-'Azzu Al-Akramu.
132. Pardoning.
133. And it is He who accepts repentance from His servants and pardons misdeeds, and He knows what you do. (Shura:25)
134. Pardon.

Allah سبحانه وتعالى has all the means and power to apply any and every retribution. Yet, Allah سبحانه وتعالى does not do it. This should be one of the examples as we take Allah سبحانه وتعالى as the Real Friend as mentioned tahalluqu bi aqlaqillah[135].

Allahumma Ja'alna Minhum. Allahu A'lam.

Yet, when one reviews the ayah { وَمَا أَصَابَكُم مِّن مُّصِيبَةٍ فَبِمَا كَسَبَتْ أَيْدِيكُمْ وَيَعْفُو عَن كَثِيرٍ {الشورى/30}[136], the case of musibahs are the filtered versions of what we normally deserve as mentioned وَيَعْفُو عَن كَثِيرٍ الشورى/٣٠}.

In another perspective, this dua is suggested to read in umrah or hajj (pilgrimage). As the person is running between two hills, the person makes istighfar and makes tawbah. Sometimes, the burden of the sins can make the person run away from his or her sins. There is no one except Allah سبحانه وتعالى to make the person reset his or position and forgive this person. Therefore, when the person commits sins constantly, developing the habit of going back to Allah سبحانه وتعالى constantly is very important and very critical.

135. Adapting the traits with how Allah SWT pleased with and Allah SWT treats all creation with mercy, caring, forgiveness and kindness.
136. And whatever strikes you of disaster—it is for what your hands have earned; but He pardons much.

32. اَللَّهُمَّ ارْحَمْنِي بِتَرْكِ الْمَعَاصِي أَبَدًا مَا أَبْقَيْتَنِي وَارْحَمْنِي أَنْ أَتَكَلَّفَ مَا لَا يَعْنِينِي وَارْزُقْنِي حُسْنَ النَّظَرِ فِيمَا يُرْضِيكَ عَنِّي[137]

O Allah! Have mercy on me, by enabling me to leave all acts of disobedience forever, as long as You preserve me. Have mercy on me, that I should not burden myself with that which does not concern me, and grant me the ability to look to what earns me Your good pleasure [5].

Sometimes, the sins that we are committing prevent us from doing good as mentioned in the expression 'Allahumma arhamni bitarkil ma'asi Abadan ma abqaytani'[138]. If one thinks about memorizing the Quran, this is one of the absolute best things to do. In this case, having this ni'mah requires purifying one's heart and mind and detaching oneself from sins constantly. If there are ones who memorized the Quran and are still involved in sins, it can be very difficult for them to keep the Quran and benefit from the Quran fully. The rule is that generally the clean and pure is with the clean and pure as mentioned:

وَالطَّيِّبَاتُ لِلطَّيِّبِينَ وَالطَّيِّبُونَ لِلطَّيِّبَاتِ أُوْلَئِكَ مُبَرَّؤُونَ مِمَّا يَقُولُونَ لَهُم مَّغْفِرَةٌ وَرِزْقٌ كَرِيمٌ {النور/26}[139]

After this disposition one can get both physical and spiritual rizq (provision) from Allah سبحانه وتعالى as mentioned وَرِزْقٌ كَرِيمٌ[140] {النور/26}.

137. Allahumma arhamni bitarkil ma'asi Abadan ma abqaytani, wa arhamni an takallafa ma la ya'neeni, wa arzuqni husna annazari fima yurdika a'nni.
138. *O Allah! Have mercy on me, by enabling me to leave all acts of disobedience forever, as long as You preserve me.*
139. Evil words are for evil men, and evil men are [subjected] to evil words. And good words are for good men, and good men are [an object] of good words
140. For them is forgiveness and noble provision.

The absolute pure and clean such as the Quran necessitates hearts and minds in a similar way. Therefore, 'malaya'gni', idle, unnecessary and pointless verbal and physical engagements may not be tolerated in the engagements of the level of memorizing the Quran and benefitting from the Quran as mentioned 'wa arhamni an takallafa ma la ya'gni'[141].

The other important part is being content always with what Allah سبحانه وتعالى gives the person and where Allah SWT puts the person in. In no case, the person should not show any displeasure with this placement and should not show any signs of displeasure or complaints in their actions, words and thoughts. This can be implied with the expression "wa arzuqni husna annazari fima yurdika a'nni[142]."

Lastly, these are all from the Rahmah and Fadl of Allah سبحانه وتعالى given to the person as mentioned and repeated with the phrase 'arhamni[143]'.

Allahuma Ja'alna minhum, amin.

(Oh Allah, make us of those people)

141. Have mercy on me, that I should not burden myself with that which does not concern me.
142. Grant me the ability to look to what earns me Your good pleasure.
143. Have mercy on me.

Difficulty—Musibah/Imtihan

33. اَللَّهُمَّ لَا سَهْلَ إِلَّا مَاجَعَلْتَهُ سَهْلًا وَأَنْتَ تَجْعَلُ الْحَزَنَ إِذَا شِئْتَ سَهْلًا[144]

O Allah! There is nothing easy except that which You make easy, and You make hardship easy if it be Your will [14].

In this dua of the Prophet ﷺ, it is important to realize that sometimes, difficulties and trials are given to us to test our disposition. In this case, if the person runs to solutions other than Allah سبحانه وتعالى, the person may not have really understood the meanings of these trials or difficulties. In other words, each trial and difficulty should be an opportunity to make a better and closer relationship with Allah سبحانه وتعالى, Rabbul A'lamin.

The above dua is an exclamation of this truth that one should first realize that Allah سبحانه وتعالى can do anything for the person. As long as the person is in this disposition truly, then the person can really understand the meanings of the trials and difficulties, Allahu A'lam.

On another perspective, this dua is very important when we are about to lose ourselves. When we are angry or when the things become overwhelming, asking for help from Allah سبحانه وتعالى can be very critical. As humans, we need to accept that we are constantly in trials or tests of decision making, facing challenges, being treated in coarse manners, and for the most part, we don't get what we want or desire most of the time in life. Considering all these, one can realize the weakness of a human and the greatness of these challenges. In all these instances, there is no way for a smart person other than asking help from Allah سبحانه وتعالى and taking refuge in Allah سبحانه وتعالى. In this perspective, one can realize how each word of this dua is very relaxing and calming the person.

---

144. Allahumma La Sahla illa ma ja'altahu sahla anta taj'alu alhazana iza she'ta sahlan.

When a person has any difficulty overpowering and exhausting the person's all energy, at these times, the human weakness and need for Allah سبحانه وتعالى can be revealed more than other times. In these perspectives, rather going around to other people and asking their help, the first disposition is to ask from Allah سبحانه وتعالى to make the difficulty easy for the person. When facing the difficulty, the person can feel anxious, fearful, uneasy, and scared. These feelings can take the person out of the calm and tranquil breezes of iman. Therefore, it is important to recite this dua in order to once more remind the person that Allah سبحانه وتعالى has the means to relieve the person from this difficulty. This dua should be constantly recited by the person if he or she wants ease in one's life.

Sometimes a person can be stuck in a situation. In this psychology, the person can become more and more stressed due to the difficulties of not getting any encouraging results. Especially when a person is working a lot but not getting results, it can put the person in a state of weakness, stress, tiredness, dizziness, and cause a lack of motivation. In this case and all others, if Allah سبحانه وتعالى makes it easy to achieve the results and if Allah سبحانه وتعالى gives barakah[145] then, the person can immediately be out of this psychology of these negative states. Therefore, this dua is very critical in one's life in order to constantly remind the person about one's human realities and the constant and continuous connection with Allah سبحانه وتعالى through dua.

One should also consider the importance of this dua in actions of doing good. Sometimes, a person may have a desire to do good. But, if the tawfik[146] of Allah سبحانه وتعالى is not there, it is not possible. Sometimes, people may desire to do something good but due to whatever reason, the person may not be able to do it. Making dua that Allah سبحانه وتعالى grants the Fadl[147] and Tawfik in executing these actions is a very critical stance as this dua also alludes to.

---

145. Blessings and easiness from Allah.
146. Help and Enablement of Allah for achieving the good and virtuous.
147. Grace.

34. اَللَّهُمَّ إِنِّي أَعُوذُ بِكَ مِنَ الْمَغْرَمِ وَالْمَأْثَمِ[148]

O Allah! I take refuge in You from the [yoke] of debt and the [burden] of sin [3].

Two things that can bother a person and cause anxiety and depression which can be due to the feelings of guilt of one's evil engagements and also the concerns about financial stability. When a person is engaged in sins, actions and evils that displease Allah سبحانه وتعالى, a person who has Iman becomes very anxious about the feelings of resentment and self-blame. Therefore, this dua can relieve the person from this burden if he or she turns fully to Allah سبحانه وتعالى and asks forgiveness for the past sins and protection from future sins.

Another source of depression and anxiety is caused by concerns regarding finances. In other words, the upcoming payments, loans, bills, debts and all other financial concerns can cause a person to fall into a real depressive state. Again, in this case, if the person turns to Allah سبحانه وتعالى with the tool of dua as thought by the Prophet ﷺ, then the burden of carrying these uneasy feelings can be removed inshAllah.

It is interesting to note that there is a similar dua about the financial concerns of debt to be recited before sleeping taught by the Prophet ﷺ [4]. One can see that these concerns can even prevent a person from sleeping or resting.

148. Allahumma inni a'uzu bika minal magrami wal ma'thami.

35. اَللّٰهُمَّ رَحْمَتَكَ أَرْجُو، فَلَا تَكِلْنِي إِلَى نَفْسِي طَرْفَةَ عَيْنٍ وَأَصْلِحْ لِي شَأْنِي كُلَّهُ لَا إِلَهَ إِلَّا أَنْتَ يَا حَيُّ يَا قَيُّومُ بِرَحْمَتِكَ أَسْتَغِيثُ[149]

O Allah! It is Your mercy that I hope for, so leave me not to myself for the blinking of an eye, and put right for me all my affairs! There is no god but You—O All—Living, Self-Subsistent [Lord]! (Ya Hayy, Ya Qayyum), in Your mercy do I seek relief [8].

The word 'rahmataka[150]' placed forward in the above sentence structure could possibly imply the emergency of Allahs سبحانه وتعالى Rahmah and the emergent need of the person for this. The person can be weak even for a second. The person can feel as if he or she is in the deep oceans of darkness. These short period engagements can put a person in very depressive and anxious states. In this perspective, is important to ask from Allah سبحانه وتعالى to rectify all our engagements. We don't know if the outcome of each of our engagements will result in something evil or good although it may look good or evil to us.

Then, true tawhid emphasizes that the person should fully turn to Allah سبحانه وتعالى for all his or her needs. Allah سبحانه وتعالى is al-Hayy[151], all the time Aware, Active, Alive and al-Qayyum[152], there is no beginning or end to the existence of Allah سبحانه وتعالى. Finally, the dua ends again with a phrase similar to the beginning phrase but with more exclamation of the need for help that the person desperately needs from the Rahmah of Allah سبحانه وتعالى, Allahu A'lam.

149. Allahumma rahmataka arju, falatakilni ila nafsi tarfata 'ayni wa aslih li sha'ni kullah la ilaha illa anta ya Hayy ya Qayyum bi rahmatika astagheethu.
150. *It is Your mercy.*
151. *O All- Living,*
152. *Self-Subsistent.*

36. اَللَّهُمَّ يَسِّرْنَا لِلْيُسْرٰى وَجَنِّبْنَا الْعُسْرٰى وَاغْفِرْ لَنَا فِي الْاٰخِرَةِ وَالْأُولٰى وَاجْعَلْنَا مِنْ أَئِمَّةِ الْمُتَّقِينَ[153]

O Allah! Facilitate our way to ease, and keep us away from hardship! Forgive us in the Hereafter, and in the here and now, and make us among the leaders of the pious!

It is important to always ask for ease from Allah سبحانه وتعالى and ask protection against the difficulties and take refuge to Allah سبحانه وتعالى. This should be the constant prayer of the person daily.

When the person is worried with different problems and responsibilities, the person can become uneasy and lose comfort and sakina (calmness). It is important to be prepared for the world means with causalities. Yet, before engaging oneself with the world of reasons, it is very critical to turn to fully to Allah سبحانه وتعالى. This dua especially reminds the person this expected disposition of a believer before engaging oneself with anything in this world.

153. Allahumma yassirna lilyusra, wa jannabna al-u'sra, wa aghfir lana fil akhirati, wal uula, wa ja'alna min aimmati al-muttaqin.

Struggles and Success—Sa'y

37. اَللَّهُمَّ اجْعَلْهُ حَجّاً مَبْرُوراً وَذَنْباً مَغْفُوراً وَسَعْياً مَشْكُوراً[154]

O Allah! Make this a blessed pilgrimage, by which my sins are forgiven, and my efforts are rewarded [10].

Above is a dua that one can perform during hajj[155] or umrah[156]. One can ask how can we benefit from all the duas of the Prophet ﷺ in other times of life and not only in specific occasions. In this case, one can see the physical struggles of life being similar to the struggles of the rituals done during Hajj or Umrah. The person can engage with oneself by making similar duas. The duas of the Prophet ﷺ have multiple folds. For example, a person exercising to be fit in order to worship Allah سبحانه وتعالى can make this dua with this intention, Allahu A'lam.

The word hajja can include some of the meanings that a person has an intention, determination with struggle and effort to achieve something. One of the most critical part of these struggles can be the result of their acceptance by Allah سبحانه وتعالى. In this regards, there is some parallelism in this dua as hajjan, zanban[157], sa'yan[158] corresponding mabruran[159], maghfuran[160], and mashkuran[161]. The first three hajjan, zanban, sa'yan belongs to the person. The last three mabruran, maghfuran, and mashkuran belongs to Allah سبحانه وتعالى. If there are no first three engagements, then there are no last three results. Sometimes there is the first three but not last three. Therefore, the person should constantly ask and be in the

154. Allahumma aj'alhu Hajjan Mabrura wa zanban maghfuran wa sa'yan mashkura.
155. Required pilgrimage
156. Optional pilgrimage
157. Sins.
158. Efforts.
159. Being *blessed.*
160. Being *forgiven.*
161. Being *rewarded.*

state of hope and fear if one's good-seeming actions are accepted by Allah سبحانه وتعالى or if it is only the person's tiredness as the Prophet ﷺ mentions that there are ones who fast but their end result is only being hungry [9]. In the Quran, similarly the verse الَّذِينَ ضَلَّ سَعْيُهُمْ فِي الْحَيَاةِ الدُّنْيَا وَهُمْ يَحْسَبُونَ أَنَّهُمْ يُحْسِنُونَ صُنْعًا {الكهف/104[162] can indicate similar failure and catastrophe of hasarah[163], while the person may think he or she is in gain, but in reality the person is in loss, may Allah سبحانه وتعالى protect us from this end, Amin.

162. They are] those whose effort is lost in worldly life, while they think that they are doing well in work. (Kahf:104)
163. Loss.

Decision Making—Istikhara

38. اَللَّهُمَّ إِنِّي أَسْتَخِيرُكَ بِعِلْمِكَ وَأَسْتَقْدِرُكَ بِقُدْرَتِكَ وَأَسْأَلُكَ مِنْ فَضْلِكَ الْعَظِيمِ، فَإِنَّكَ تَقْدِرُ وَلَا أَقْدِرُ وَتَعْلَمُ وَلَا أَعْلَمُ وَأَنْتَ عَلَّامُ الْغُيُوبِ.[164]

اللَّهُمَّ إِنْ كُنْتَ تَعْلَمُ أَنَّ هَذَا الأَمْرَ خَيْرٌ لِي فِي دِينِي، وَمَعَاشِي، وَعَاقِبَةِ أَمْرِي أَوْ عَاجِلِ أَمْرِي وَآجِلِهِ، فَاقْدُرْهُ لِي وَيَسِّرْهُ لِي ثُمَّ بَارِكْ لِي فِيهِ، وَإِنْ كُنْتَ تَعْلَمُ أَنَّ هَذَا الْأَمْرَ شَرٌّ لِي فِي دِينِي وَمَعَاشِي وَعَاقِبَةِ أَمْرِي أَوْ فِي عَاجِلِ أَمْرِي وَآجِلِهِ، فَاصْرِفْهُ عَنِّي وَاصْرِفْنِي عَنْهُ، وَاقْدُرْ لِي الْخَيْرَ حَيْثُ كَانَ، ثُمَّ أَرْضِنِي[165]

O Allah! I seek Your guidance in my choice, by virtue of Your knowledge, and I seek ability from You by virtue of Your power. I ask You out of Your great favor, for You have power, but I have none, and You know, but I know not, and You are the Knower of the unseen O Allah, if You know that this matter is good for me with regard to my religion, my livelihood and the end of my affair then decree it for me, facilitate it for me, and grant me blessing in it. And if You know that this matter is not good for me with regard to my religion, my livelihood and the end of my affair then turn it away from me and me from it; and decree for me better than it, wherever it may be, and make me content with it." [3].

This dua is very critical in its wording. It places the person in its real disposition of Iman. In other words, the person is required to implement all the faculties of iman at all times. In this case, a person admits first as a weak creation and a human being that he or she does not know anything in reality except when the person is guided by Allah سبحانه وتعالى. The person cannot do anything in reality except when the person is empowered by Allah سبحانه

164. Allahumma inni astakhiruka biilmika wa astaqdiruka biqudratik wa asaluka min fadlikaal 'aziim, fainnaka taqdiru, wa la aqdiru, wa ta'lamu, wa la a'lamu, wa anta 'Allamul Guyub.
165. Allâhumma in kunta ta'lamu anna hâdhal amra khayrun li fi dini wa ma-ashi wa aqibati amri faqdir-hu li wa yassir-hu li thumma barik li fihi wa in kunta ta'lamu anna hâdhal amra sharrun li fi dini wa maâshi wa aqibati amri fasrifhu anni wasrifni anhu waqdir liyal-khayra haythu kâna thumma ardini.

وتعالى. It is similar to a machine. The machine will sit there until it is plugged into an electric outlet, then machine can move, make sounds and properly function according to the purpose for which it is designed for. Similarly, a human is a cold, physical body. He or she can act according to their designed and created purpose once they are connected to Allah سبحانه وتعالى. Self-confident acts or attitudes are all lies. Forgetting Allah سبحانه وتعالى in all engagements implicitly are all invitations for unfruitful, unsuccessful and failure outcomes to teach and remind the person this real purpose of their design and real purpose. Therefore, the dua of istikhara is very critical in this sense before making any engagements.

39. اَللَّهُمَّ اهْدِنِي بِالْهُدٰى وَنَقِّنِي بِالتَّقْوٰى وَاغْفِرْ لِي فِي الْاٰخِرَةِ وَالْأُولٰى[166]

O Allah! Lead me with Your guidance, cleanse me with piety, and forgive me in the Hereafter and in this life.

One can see in the above dua that hidayah[167] is a process. We are required to constantly ask for hidayah in Surah Fatiha by reading it seventeen times a day in the obligatory prayers. This can be that a person's state of heart and mind can be constantly changing.

This change can be seen in two ways. The person can be losing this hidayah and asking Allah سبحانه وتعالى again and again to restore it.

Or, the person can be linearly increasing one's hidayah until he or she dies. The expected state of one's hidayah after one minute should be higher than a minute before. In other words, a person should be closer to Allah سبحانه وتعالى compared to a minute ago through the constant asking of hidayah from Allah سبحانه وتعالى. So, our hidayah should not be stagnant but we should be changing, increasing and perfecting it as much as possible until we die.

On another note, hidayah could be the initial entrance similar to turning the key of a car. Taqwa (God-consciousness) is the process of increasing the quality and quantity of this hidayah.

---

166. Allahumm ahdini bil huda, wa naqqini, bittaqwa, waghfirli fil aakhirati wal uula.
167. Guidance.

Sickness—Shifa

40. اَللَّهُمَّ مَتِّعْنِي بِبَصَرِي وَاجْعَلْهُ الْوَارِثَ مِنِّي وَأَرِنِي فِي الْعَدُوِّ ثَأْرِي وَانْصُرْنِي عَلَى مَنْ ظَلَمَنِي[168]

O Allah, let me enjoy my sight and keep this faculty intact and healthy show me the fulfillment of my vengeance upon my enemy and help me against whoever has wronged me! [5]

It is interesting to see there is a specific dua for the pains of eye. It is a specific dua for the full usage of the eyes in one's health. A person who is on the path to Allah سبحانه وتعالى can sleep less and can possibly be exposed to the evil of others. Therefore, there can be an effect on the person, Allahu Alam. In this regard, the second part of this dua expresses protection from external effects.

41. بِسْمِ اللهِ، بِسْمِ اللهِ، بِسْمِ اللهِ، أَعُوذُ بِعِزَّةِ اللهِ وَقُدْرَتِهِ مِنْ شَرِّ مَا أَجِدُ وَأُحَاذِرُ مِنْ وَجَعِي هٰذَا[169]

In the name of Allah, in the name of Allah, in the name of Allah, I take refuge in the Might and Power of Allah from the malevolence of this pain that I am experiencing and that is troubling me [5].

The above is the dua of the Prophet ﷺ for the one who is having pain in any part of his or her body. The person puts one's hand where the source of the pain is and reads this dua.

168. Allahumma matta'ni bibasari wa ja'lhul waritha minni, wa arini fil a'duwwi tha'ri, wa ansurni a'la man zalamani.
169. Bismillah, bismillah, bismillah, au'uzu bi'izzatillahi, wa qudratihi min sharri ma ajidu wa ahaziru min waja'i haza.

In this dua, one can self-treat the ailment with the recitation of this expression. Starting everything with the name of Allah سبحانه وتعالى is the key. Then, for whatever reason this sickness has affected this person, one ought to seek refuge in Allah سبحانه وتعالى from it. Then, for whatever reason this sickness touches the person, taking refuge in Allah سبحانه وتعالى who is All-Powerful and All-Control of everything and asking protection from the evils of this situation and asking refrainment, avoidance from the pain and cure for the pain are some important notions to understand.

42. اَللّٰهُمَّ أَذْهِبِ الْبَأْسَ رَبَّ النَّاسِ، اِشْفِ أَنْتَ الشَّافِي لَا شِفَاءَ إِلَّا شِفَاؤُكَ شِفَاءً لَا يُغَادِرُ سَقَمًا[170]

Take away the harm, Lord of men! Heal! For You are the All-Healer; there is no cure save Your cure, and leave him without a trace of sickness! [3]

It is important to know and accept who is the Real Curer, Ash-Shafi. One can follow the sabab (means) because following the causality is following the system that Allah سبحانه وتعالى created.

إِنَّا مَكَّنَّا لَهُ فِي الْأَرْضِ وَآتَيْنَاهُ مِن كُلِّ شَيْءٍ سَبَبًا {الكهف/٨٤} فَأَتْبَعَ سَبَبًا {الكهف/85}. [171]

Therefore, according to the opinions of some scholars, not following the causes created by Allah سبحانه وتعالى can be a disrespect to the system and order that Allah سبحانه وتعالى created [15].

---

170. Allahumma azhib al-ba'sa, Rabbinnas!, ishfi, Anta Shaafi!, la shifaa'a, illa shifaauka, shifaauka shifa'an la yughaadiru saqaman.

171. Indeed, We established him upon the earth, and We gave him to everything a way [i.e., means]. So he followed a means. (Kahf:84-85)

43. اَللَّهُمَّ اشْفِ عَبْدَكَ يَنْكَأُ لَكَ عَدُوًّا أَوْ يَمْشِي لَكَ إِلَى جَنَازَةٍ[172]

"O Allah, cure Your seeker, and worshipper" who tries to stop the oppressors and evil-doers for Your Sake and who attends to funeral prayers of the deceased for Your sake [8].

From this dua of the Prophet saw, one can recite the good deeds of the person while asking shifa, cure for the person from Allah سبحانه وتعالى. This dua can teach us to make dua to this person by using the shafa'a of a good deed of this person. This approach can be realized also in the case of three people stuck in a cave with a rock closing the entrance [4] (2743). Then, they make dua to Allah سبحانه وتعالى by mentioning their good deeds so that the calamity can be removed from them.

Another example can be that if the sick person memorized a page from Surah Al-I Imran and other surahs, a person can make dua to Allah سبحانه وتعالى for the sake of those surah surahs or pages that this person memorized. One can extend this approach making dua to a person by presenting other good deeds performed by this person, Allahu A'lam.

172. Allahumma ashfi 'abddaka yankau laka 'aduwwan aw yamshi laka ila janazatin.

Daily Engagements—Mubasharat

44. اَللّٰهُمَّ إِنِّي أَسْأَلُكَ خَيْرَهَا وَخَيْرَ مَا جَبَلْتَهَا عَلَيْهِ وَأَعُوذُ بِكَ مِنْ شَرِّهَا وَشَرِّ مَا جَبَلْتَهَا عَلَيْهِ[173]

O Allah! Verily I ask of You its goodness, and the goodness that You molded it with, and I seek refuge in You from its evil and the evil that You molded it with [8].

As everything can either be a nimah or test, it is always important to understand the dual identity of everything as a possible source of evil or good for the person. Therefore, the person should constantly ask with humbleness and humility for Tawfik, Fadl and Rahmah of Allah سبحانه وتعالى. Iman is the disposition of attitude of humbleness and humility in front of Rabbul A'lamin.

45. اللّٰهُمَّ إِنِّي أَسْأَلُكَ خَيْرَ الْمَوْلَجِ، وَخَيْرَ الْمَخْرَجِ، بِاسْمِ اللّٰهِ وَلَجْنَا وَبِاسْمِ اللّٰهِ خَرَجْنَا، وَعَلَى اللّٰهِ رَبِّنَا تَوَكَّلْنَا[174]

O Allah! Verily I ask of You the goodness of coming and entering, and the goodness of leaving and exiting. With the Name of Allah, we enter. With the Name of Allah, we exit and leave. We fully rely and trust on our Sustainer, Nourisher, our Rabb, Allah. [8].

As we enter or leave a place to be in a gathering, to spend time with family, or take care of a business, simple looking reminders like this dua can transform all our engagements into the ones with much fruitful and less stressful pleasant outcomes. The duas like this one make us to remind ourselves the awareness of our intention before we lose ourselves in the midst of these engagements.

Asking Allah سبحانه وتعالى for protection from the evil of the gatherings and asking good of them is important as mentioned in this dua.

---

173. Allahumma inni asaluka khayraha, khayra ma jabaltaha alayhi, wa au'zu bika min sharriha, wa sharri ma jabaltaha alayhi.

174. Allahumma inni asaluka khayraha, khayral mawlaja, wa khayral makhraja, bismillah walaja'na, wa bismillahi, kharajna, wa 'ala-Allahi Rabbina tawakkalna.

Fear—Khawf

46. اَللهُ أَكْبَرُ اَللهُ أَكْبَرُ، اَللهُ أَعَزُّ مِنْ خَلْقِهِ جَمِيعًا، اَللهُ أَعَزُّ مِمَّا أَخَافُ وَأَحْذَرُ، أَعُوذُ بِاللهِ الَّذِي لَا إِلٰهَ إِلَّا هُوَ الْمُمْسِكُ السَّمَاءِ أَنْ تَقَعَ عَلَى الْأَرْضِ إِلَّا بِإِذْنِهِ مِنْ شَرِّ عَبْدِكَ... (يسمي) وَجُنُودِهِ وَأَتْبَاعِهِ وَأَشْيَاعِهِ مِنَ الْجِنِّ وَالْإِنْسِ، اَللَّهُمَّ كُنْ لِي جَارًا مِنْ شَرِّهِمْ، جَلَّ ثَنَاؤُكَ، وَعَزَّ جَارُكَ، وَلَا إِلٰهَ غَيْرُكَ (٣)[175]

Allah is the Greatest! Allah is the Greatest! Allah is Mightier than all of His creation! Allah is Mightier than all that I fear and am wary of! I take refuge in Allah—besides Whom there is no other god, Who keeps [what is in] the sky from falling onto the earth, save [that it should occur] by His leave—from the mischief of Your creation . . . (one names the person/thing that he/she is scared/afraid of). [I take refuge] from his soldiers, his followers and his partisans from amongst jinn and men. O Allah! Be my redeemer from their malevolence. Exalted is Your praise! Honored is Your protégé! There is no god but You. [3] (three times)

It is always important ask protection from Allah سبحانه وتعالى from the trials, hasad and tribulations coming from people. In the above prayer, one first remembers who Allah سبحانه وتعالى is. This is a way of refreshing one's iman (faith). In reality, when a person has a true iman, then this person is not scared of anything or anyone. Then, in the second part of this dua, the person specifically mentions the name of the person or thing that he or she is scared of. This is similar to a spiritual surgery, removing a specific or localized disease or tumor in the body. In the last part of the dua, the person again refreshes their iman and charges oneself with the expected true relationship with Allah سبحانه وتعالى.

---

175. Allahu Akbar, Allahu a'azzu min khalqihi jami'an, Allahu a'azzu mimma akhafu wa ahzaru, a'uzu billahi allazi la ilaha illa huwa almumsika assamai an taqaa' a'lal ardi illa biiznihi min sharri a'bdika (mentioning the name of the person that the person/thing is scared from), wa junudihi, wa atbai'hi, wa ashya'ihi minal jinni, wal insi, Allahumma kun li jaaran min sharrihim, Jalla thanauk, wa a'zza jaaruka, wa la ilaha ghayruk.

Sadness & Grief—Hazan

47. اَللَّهُمَّ إِنِّي أَعُوذُ بِكَ مِنَ الْهَمِّ وَالْحَزَنِ وَأَعُوذُ بِكَ مِنَ الْعَجْزِ وَالْكَسَلِ وَأَعُوذُ بِكَ مِنَ
الْجُبْنِ وَالْبُخْلِ وَأَعُوذُ بِكَ مِنْ غَلَبَةِ الدَّيْنِ وَقَهْرِ الرِّجَالِ[176] (٣)

O Allah! I seek refuge in You from worry and grief, and I seek refuge in You from incapacity and sloth. I seek refuge in You from cowardice and miserliness and I seek refuge in You from overpowering debt and subjugation by men [3] *(three times).*

If we analyze our typical day, we wake up, then during the day until we sleep, our feelings constantly change. One of these feelings is "hamm", the sadness and grief about the past events and "hazan" the worries about future. The present or anytime of emotions of the person can be combined and formed with both hamm and hazan, the sadness and grief about the past and fears and worries about the future. These anytime feelings can be amplified with a gloomy dark weather, with a bad smell, a bad word or with other factors. With all these dynamically changing feelings and emotions, one can really deteriorate and injure oneself. Injuries on the spirit, soul and ruh and qalb and heart can be more deadly than the injuries on the body. Injuries on our ruh and qalb gauges and makes the person to execute decisions. They make us form our intentions and finalize our choices in life. If the ruh and qalb are not sound then these executions leading to actions will not be sound. Rasulullah ﷺ mentions that there is a piece of flesh in the body if it is sound then everything is sound, that is the heart [3] [4].

176. Allahumma inn au'zu bika minal hammi wal hazan, wa a'uzu bika minal a'jzi wal kasal, wa a'uzu bika minal jubni wal bukhl, wa a'uzu bika min ghalabati addayni wa qahrir rijali.

In this regard, this dua is an immediate cure for the person. When there is any pain in the person's body, it is very common to take a Tylenol or ibuprofen without any prescription over the counter. Similarly, this dua is immediately accessible. This dua is a cure and medicine that can be effective for any type of pain that is generally caused in the person's heart and ruh with fear, anxiety, sadness and worries, SubhanAllah.

Alhamdullilahi Allazi ala' ni'matil Islam[177].

Knowledge—'Ilm

48. اللَّهُمَّ إِنِّي أَسْأَلُكَ عِلْمًا نَافِعًا وَرِزْقًا طَيِّبًا وَعَمَلاً مُتَقَبِّلاً[178]

O Allah! I ask and request from You a beneficial knowledge, pure nourishment and accepted occupations of Your Pleasure [14].

The purpose of sleeping and getting up with a new energy can indicate using this energy for betterment of one's relationship with Allah سبحانه وتعالى. This can be fully realized and embodied especially with acquiring and increasing one's knowledge. Rasulullah ﷺ read the above dua after fajr (morning) prayer.

As mentioned in some other versions similar to this dua, acquiring useful and relevant knowledge (i'lm) can be the purpose and goal in one's life. In this dua and others, the word useful and relevant (nafia') is specifically mentioned. In other words, an unused knowledge can always be distraction for the person. One can especially observe this today. The importance of "relevancy" is increasingly emphasized in our public school curriculums by the state education departments. In other words, the students or adults learn a knowledge or choose a discipline if they have the potential to apply it in different parts of their life.

177. All praise and gratitude is fully due and credited to Allah for the blessing of Islam.
178. Allahumma innee as-aluka 'ilman naafi'anw wrizqant tayyibanw wa 'amalan mutqabbalaa

Blessings—Barakah

49. اَللَّهُمَّ اعْصِمْنِي مِنَ الشَّيْطَانِ، اَللَّهُمَّ إِنِّيَ أَسْأَلُكَ مِنْ فَضْلِكَ[179]

O Allah! Grant me protection from Satan. O Allah! I ask of You Your favor [4].

This dua is recommended especially to say and embody when one is leaving the masjid. The person can become more vulnerable to the attacks of evil outside compared to the places of dhikr, where the remembrance of Allah سبحانه وتعالى is practiced. These could be masjid, mosques or other places depending on the quantity and quality levels of how true remembrance of Allah سبحانه وتعالى is practiced.

One can realize that the Fadl and Rahmah of Allah سبحانه وتعالى can descend on the person when the person is engaged spending time in the masjid by attending the jamaah and other dhikrs, Allahu A'lam.

50. اَللَّهُمَّ إِنَّا نَسْأَلُكَ مُوجِبَاتِ رَحْمَتِكَ وَعَزَائِمَ مَغْفِرَتِكَ وَالسَّلَامَةَ مِنْ كُلِّ إِثْمٍ وَالْغَنِيمَةَ مِنْ كُلِّ بِرٍّ وَالْفَوْزَ بِالْجَنَّةِ وَالنَّجَاةَ مِنَ النَّارِ[180]

O Allah! Truly we ask You for the means of deserving Your mercy, the means of being certain of Your forgiveness, protection from every sin, the benefit of every virtue, the triumph of Paradise, and deliverance from the Hellfire [16].

When the person is in need the person can turn to Allah سبحانه وتعالى with full embodiment of submission. At that point, when the Rahmah[181] and blessings of Allah سبحانه وتعالى coincides with the

179. Allahumma a'simni minas shaytani, Allahumm inni asaluka min fadlik.
180. Allahumma inna nasaluka mujibaati rahmatik, wa 'azaima maghfiratika, wassalamata min kulli ithmin wal ghanimata min Kulli birrin, wal fawza bil jannati wa najata min annari.
181. Mercy.

sincere disposition of this person, then different doors can open for the person. But one should not forget that every blessing can turn into a trial or test if the person does not know how to detach oneself from everything except Allah سبحانه وتعالى. Constantly asking and begging for the Rahmah of Allah سبحانه وتعالى in order to have easiness in life is important although the person may be engaged in a lot of things that is against the pleasure of Allah سبحانه وتعالى.

51. اَللَّهُمَّ قَنِّعْنِي بِمَا رَزَقْتَنِي وَبَارِكْ لِي فِيهِ وَاخْلُفْ عَلَى كُلِّ غَائِبَةٍ لِي بِخَيْرٍ[182]

O Allah! Make me content with that with which You have provided me; bless me by it, and recompense those I have left behind with goodness [16] [17]!

One of the concerns that causes a person to be overwhelmed in life is monetary or financial issues. Sometimes, this worry, or concern can defocus the person from his or her real purpose in life. One of the things that make the early generations, especially the sahabah, distinctive compared to the later generations was that Rasulullah ﷺ taught them how to be worry free from these concerns and they implemented them in their lives. One of the key words in this dua is 'qanaa'h, which means to be content and happy with what Allah سبحانه وتعالى gave the person but not looking at the people of higher wealth and world status. If a person does not have 'qanaa'h', then the person can be uneasy, and not content with what one has. The latter key word is 'barakah' in this dua. When Allah سبحانه وتعالى gives barakah to someone in their life or puts barakah in something, then SubhanAllah big things can happen with little efforts and sincere intentions.

---

182. Allahumma qanni'ni bima razaqtani, barikli fiihi, wa khalluf a'la kulli ghaibatin lii bikhayrin.

Helplessness and Weakness—Hawl and Quwwah

52. يَا حَيُّ يَا قَيُّومُ بِرَحْمَتِكَ أَسْتَغِيثُ أَصْلِحْ لِي شَأْنِي كُلَّهُ وَلَا تَكِلْنِي إِلَى نَفْسِي طَرْفَةَ عَيْنٍ[183]

(O All-Living, Self-Subsistent [Lord]!) Ya Hayyu Ya Qayyum! For the sake of Your Mercy I beg for help. Rectify for all my states and leave me not to myself even for the blinking of an eye! [5]

As the person constantly goes through daily ups and downs, this dua is very critical to accept one's true disposition in front of Allah سبحانه وتعالى that the person is weak and helpless unless there is help from Allah سبحانه وتعالى. On the other hand, sometimes the person can be in virtuous and good-seeming engagements and actions yet, the person can have dispositions and engagements that may be displeasing Allah سبحانه وتعالى. Therefore, the second portion of this dua as "aslihli sha'ni kulluh wa la takilni ila nafsi tarfata ay'n[184]."

When the person is in need of constant intervention in one's life, the Names of Allah سبحانه وتعالى الْحَيُّ الْقَيُّوم saves the person from the oppression and darkness of each second. Therefore, the dua of the Prophet ﷺ "Ya Hayy Ya Qayyum Bi Rahmatika Astaghiz,[185] Aslihli Kulli Shay wa la takilni nafsi ila tarfata a'ynin[186]" shows the need of constant connection with Allah سبحانه وتعالى at the level of each second or even each minimal time quantity. From another perspective, this shows that the person should be

---

183. Ya Hayy, Ya Qayyum, bi Rahmatik!, Astaghithus, aslihli sha'ni kullah, wa la takilni ila nafsii tarfata a'yni.

184. *Rectify for all my states and leave me not to myself even for the blinking of an eye!*

185. *(O All-Living, Self-Subsistent [Lord]!) Ya Hayyu Ya Qayyum! For the sake of Your Mercy I beg for help.*

186. *Rectify for all my states and leave me not to myself even for the blinking of an eye!*

constantly self-dealing with him or herself to check the existence of this connection and to refresh this connection with Allah سبحانه وتعالى. This could be similar to symbols on cell phones showing the level of connection or no connection. Each disconnection with Allah سبحانه وتعالى is a darkness, a black hole, and a seed for depression, darkness and anxiety. Then, other duas of the Prophet ﷺ as "Allahumma sabit Qalbi ala dinika[187]," complements this important notion.

The person is constantly in need of Allah سبحانه وتعالى. Sometimes, the need comes because there are a lot of people who may need help but the person cannot help them and asks from the One Who has the source of all help. When sometimes people see the situation of themselves, people or situations that she or he cannot do anything about, then at this point, calling Allah سبحانه وتعالى "Ya Hayy Ya Qayyum[188]" can open the doors and break all the knots of these depressing and overwhelming cases, subhanAllah.

As we are humans we are constantly in need of help. We ask help for our own selves. We ask help for others. Sometimes, a person sees or hears situation constantly, over and over but the person is helpless cannot do anything about it. He or she gets sad and feels down, and sometimes, gets depressed and disheartened. He or she may do an effort or something in that effect. Yet, he or she knows that its effect can be like an ant's effort. Again at this point, before and after, all the time, when the person makes this dua "Ya Hayy Ya Qayyum Astaghisu[189]," they should remember that Allah سبحانه وتعالى, the of All Help and All Power, can change everything.

---

187. Oh Allah! Fix and stabilize my heart on Your religion.
188. *(O All-Living, Self-Subsistent [Lord]!) Ya Hayyu Ya Qayyum! For the sake of Your Mercy I beg for help.*
189. *(O All-Living, Self-Subsistent [Lord]!) Ya Hayyu Ya Qayyum! For the sake of Your Mercy I beg for help.*

When especially all the duas including this dua are accompanied with tears and sincerity, then definitely, Allah SWT answers all the calls as Allah سبحانه وتعالى is As-Sami', the One Who Hears and al-Mujibu Adda'waat, the True Answerer of all callings or prayers.

In this dua, there can be two great Names of Allah سبحانه وتعالى as al-Hayy[190] and al-Qayyum[191] and at the same time the humility and nothingness of humans and asking help with 'astaghisu' are all present in this dua. When this is truly and sincerely embodied by the person, then this person can move mountains, speak with the dead and get an immeasurable power from Allah سبحانه وتعالى and with the permission of Allah سبحانه وتعالى.

The existence of miracles by the Prophets are some examples of this true embodiment of this disposition by the humans. Even, if this was embodied by the salaf, the righteous presiders or people, then this effect can still be there, inshAllah.

---

190. One of the Names and Attributes of Allah. One of the translations can be "the One Who is All-Alive and All-Active, the Source of all lives." This Name is considered as one of the greatest Names of Allah.
191. One of the Names and Attributes of Allah. One of the translations can be "the One Who is All- Continuously Alive and Active without beginning and end, the Permanent and the Forever." This Name is considered as one of the greatest Names of Allah.

53. اَللَّهُمَّ إِنِّي أَشْكُو إِلَيْكَ ضَعْفَ قُوَّتِي وَقِلَّةَ حِيلَتِي وَهَوَانِي عَلَى النَّاسِ[192]

O Allah! Truly do I complain to You of my lack of strength and ability, and my ineffectualness with people [17].

When the person embodies his or her weakness that one cannot do anything without the enablement of Allah سبحانه وتعالى, then this dua can open itself to the person. In other words, for example, a person in old age, sicknesses or with other health problems, or with no strength and other weaknesses, can make the person fully turn to Allah سبحانه وتعالى. In its essence, in some of the tariqahs[193], faqr and ajz[194] are desired states to reach in front of Allah سبحانه وتعالى. With this state of weakness, when the person turns to Allah سبحانه وتعالى, all the doors can open and the person can become the strongest person on the earth, Allahu A'lam.

54. اَللَّهُمَّ أَعِنَّا عَلَى ذِكْرِكَ وَشُكْرِكَ وَحُسْنِ عِبَادَتِكَ[195]

O Allah! Assist us in remembering You, showing gratitude toward You, and worshipping You properly! [8]

It is important to ask Allah سبحانه وتعالى to allow us to enjoy our prayers and ibadah[196] performed for Allah سبحانه وتعالى. In this perspective, one should use this dua to beg Allah سبحانه وتعالى that the fardh[197] prayers, tahajjud[198], fasting, and old others become the person's nature with easiness, pleasure, and joy. In other words, the person takes pleasure in praying but does not only see it as a requirement to fulfill. Allahumma ja'alna minhum, amin.

---

192. Allahumma inni ashku ilayka da'fa quwwati, wa qillata hiylati, wa hawani a'la annasi.
193. Spiritual paths in Sufism.
194. Spiritual poverty, helplessness, and weakness.
195. Allahumma ainni ala zikrika wa shukrika wa husni ibadatika.
196. Worship.
197. Required prayers.
198. Night optional but strongly suggested prayers performed by the Prophet Muhammad (saw).

55. حَسْبِيَ اللهُ لاَ إِلَٰهَ إِلاَّ هُوَ عَلَيْهِ تَوَكَّلْتُ وَهُوَ رَبُّ الْعَرْشِ الْعَظِيمِ[199]

Allah is my sufficiency, there is no god but Allah. In Allah have I put my trust and Allah is the Sustainer and Nourisher of the Noble Authority. (Tawba 9:129). [1]

The dua of Rasulullah ﷺ as also mentioned in the Quran (9:129) as 'Hasbiya Allahu, la ilaha illa hu, a'layhi tawakkultu, wa huwa Rabbul A'rshil A'ziim' is one of the duas to be read regularly to remind a person of the reality. This reality is that humans are weak. For a few seconds, we can feel good and happy. Then immediately after, we can get feelings of anxiety, fear or uneasiness that are related with unknowns, or anything we fear from due to the consequence of our actions and decisions. Therefore, when the person knows Allah سبحانه وتعالى can do anything as mentioned إِنَّ اللهَ عَلَى كُلِّ شَيْءٍ قَدِيرٌ {البقرة/٢٠}[200], then one remembers this easing point of aqidah with this dua. This disposition leads the mu'min to ease and tawakkul but at the same time leads the munafiq (the hypocrite) or kafir (the ungrateful) to fear, hopelessness and anxiety.

---

199. Hasbiya Allahu, la ilaha illa hu, a'layhi tawakkultu, wa huwa Rabbul A'rshil A'ziim.

200. Indeed, Allah is over all things competent.

Changing Conditions & Evil Change—Istiqamah

56. يَا مُقَلِّبَ الْقُلُوبِ، ثَبِّتْ قَلْبِي عَلَى دِينِكَ [201]

O Allah, Changer of hearts! Bind my heart to Your religion [5].

This is a very commonly recited, simple looking but very critical and important dua. In different discourses of day, a person is constantly fluctuating with one's relationship with Allah سبحانه وتعالى. A person's own nafs and external affects from people or shayateen can make things very difficult to surf in the peaceful waves of iman[202]. A person generally asks why in Ramadan there is still evil although the shayateens[203] are held back? The answer is simple. In Ramadan, the real untrained nafs[204] reveals itself as nafs-ammara[205] with its raw and evil tendencies. Therefore, if an evil occurs in Ramadan, it is mostly the person's true self revealing itself. Therefore, the person should really use this as an opportunity to know his or her real self and work on it. In this perspective, this dua makes the help of Allah سبحانه وتعالى to be very critical for the person in all different types of their weaknesses towards his or her real self.

One should constantly monitor his or her heart and have the fear that at any time with any incident the heart can change to the wrong direction other than Allah سبحانه وتعالى.

---

201. Ya Muqallibal Quluub, thabiit qalbii a'la dinika.
202. Belief.
203. Satans.
204. Ego or self. There is an untrained nafs called nafs-ammara. This nafs or ego can ride on the person like a horse. This ego can control the person and can make the person do evil. There are other types of nafs that the person can ride on their ego and this can then be called self instead of ego. This self can be in control of his or her ego partially or fully. In the quality and quantity of this control, there are different classifications and namings. These can be nafs-lawwamah, the blaming self with repentance and regret, nafs-mutmainnah, the happy self in their relationship with Allah, and nafs-radiyyah, the fully pleased and satisfied self in their relationship with Allah.
205. Raw and evil untrained ego.

57. رَبَّنَا لَا تُزِغْ قُلُوبَنَا بَعْدَ إِذْ هَدَيْتَنَا وَهَبْ لَنَا مِنْ لَدُنْكَ رَحْمَةً إِنَّكَ أَنتَ الْوَهَّابُ[206]
{آل عمران/8}

"O our Sustainer! Let not our hearts swerve from the truth after Thou hast guided us; and bestow upon us the gift of Thy grace: verily, Thou art the [true] Giver of Gifts [2].

This dua can especially help the person when it comes to the burden of uncertainty of one's real inner state with Allah سبحانه وتعالى. In other words, being on the siratul-mustaqim[207] is one hundred percent due to the Fadl and Rahmah of Allah سبحانه وتعالى. In this regard, if one analyzes the word hablana[208] and the Name of Allah سبحانه وتعالى al-Wahhab[209], one can indicate this notion that guidance, hidayah, and being on siratul-mustaqim[210] is not due to one's piety or anything else but solely given by Allah سبحانه وتعالى. When Prophet Yusuf mentions تَوَفَّنِي مُسْلِمًا وَأَلْحِقْنِي بِالصَّالِحِينَ[211, 212] يوسف/101}, then one can realize this uncertainty of one's ending until he or she dies. Therefore, one should constantly ask from al-Wahhab for this hidayah, and guidance, regardless of one's amal (actions). Amalu-salih[213] inshAllah can bring the tawajjuh, Fadl, and Rahmah of Allah سبحانه وتعالى on us. Yet, Allah سبحانه وتعالى is al-Wahhab gives without any means, reasons or exchange.

---

206. Rabbna la tuzi'gh qulubuna ba'da iz hadaytana wa hablana min ladunka rahmatan, Innaka Antal Wahhab.
207. Straight and correct path. Being on straight path, meaning following the Divine Guidance incessantly and continuously.
208. *Bestow upon us.*
209. *The [true] Giver of Gifts.*
210. Being on straight path, meaning following the Divine Guidance incessantly and continuously.
211. Tawaffani Musliman alhiqni bi Salihin.
212. Cause me to die a Muslim and join me with the righteous, (Yusuf:101).
213. Good and virtuous actions accepted by Allah

58. اَللّٰهُمَّ اعْصِمْنَا بِدِينِكَ وَطَوَاعِيَتِكَ وَطَوَاعِيَةِ رَسُولِكَ ﷺ وَجَنِّبْنَا حُدُودَكَ[214]

O Allah! Protect us through [adherence to] Your religion, through obedience to You and Your Messenger (peace and blessings be upon him); and keep us from [transgressing] the limits You have prescribed! [18]

Asking Allah سبحانه وتعالى for guidance to do what is pleasing to Allah سبحانه وتعالى and following the Sunnah of Rasulullah ﷺ by not approaching the boundaries is very important. We cannot take anything on our weak shoulders and expect all good to come from Allah سبحانه وتعالى, another avenue where we need to realize our weakness. Our abilities, willpower, weakness/strength, and needs constantly change. If one does not rely on Allah سبحانه وتعالى and ask seek istighfar (forgiveness) at the times of crossing boundaries, then the person can crack his or her back by making zulm (oppression) on oneself.

As the person goes through the cycles of the day, hour and even sometimes the minutes, there is no certainty, guarantee, or safety that the person can be safe from displeasing Allah سبحانه وتعالى. Therefore, the word "deen" is called these teachings including the pleasures and displeasures of Allah سبحانه وتعالى. In this regard, application of these teachings are critical to safeguard one's iman. Iman itself is not sufficient without amal. In other words, amal helps and solidifies the disposition of iman. Yet, the person is weak. It is important for us to ask help from Allah سبحانه وتعالى for the enablement of utilizing these dynamics of iman in amal.

On the other hand, asking protection from the pitfalls of the waswasa, bad-thoughts, and wrong emotional and idea based renderings coming externally and internally are very critical.

---

214. Allahumma a'simna bidinika wa taawa'yatika wa tawaa'yati Rasulika wa janibna hududak.

To summarize, asking from Allah سبحانه وتعالى for the correct iman, increasing the iman and protecting it by the help of Allah سبحانه وتعالى is paramount. Yet, at the same time, asking Allah سبحانه وتعالى for the help of doing regular and correct a'mal that Allah سبحانه وتعالى is pleased is another complementary point.

59. اَللَّهُمَّ اقْسِمْ لَنَا مِنْ خَشْيَتِكَ مَا تَحُولُ بِهِ بَيْنَنَا وَبَيْنَ مَعَاصِيكَ وَمِنْ طَاعَتِكَ مَا تُبَلِّغُنَا بِهِ جَنَّتَكَ وَمِنَ الْيَقِينِ مَا تُهَوِّنُ بِهِ عَلَيْنَا مَصَائِبَ الدُّنْيَا وَمَتِّعْنَا بِأَسْمَاعِنَا وَأَبْصَارِنَا وَقُوَّتِنَا مَا أَحْيَيْتَنَا[215]

O Allah! Apportion to us fear of You which obstructs us from Your disobedience, obedience to You by which we gain Your Paradise, and certainty that makes it easy for us to endure the afflictions of this life. Let us enjoy our hearing, sight, and strength as long as You keep us alive [5].

Sometimes, we go through different emotional cycles during the day. The feelings of joy, happiness, and satisfaction can be deadly in our relationship with Allah سبحانه وتعالى and people. When the person does not have sufficient 'khasyah[216]' with Allah سبحانه وتعالى, then this can make the person disrespectful with Allah سبحانه وتعالى. The feeling of arrogance can be the sign of insufficient khasyah in a person. A person cannot be self-satisfied truly in this dunya (world) due to not knowing where he or she will end up after death.

This dua has critical stance in this sense because the person asks Allah سبحانه وتعالى for a sufficient khasyah[217] in order to not be arrogant and lose what he or she has built up in their relationship with Allah سبحانه وتعالى.

---

215. Allahumma aqsimlana min khashyatika ma tahulu bihi baynana wa bayna ma'siika, wa min taa'tika ma tublighuna bihi jannataka, wa minal yaqini ma tuhwwinu bihi a'layna masaaiba addunya, wa matta'na bi asmaai'na, wa absarina, wa quwwatina ma ahyaytana.
216. Respect for Allah.
217. Respect for Allah.

60. اَللَّهُمَّ أَلْهِمْنِي رُشْدِي وَأَعِذْنِي مِنْ شَرِّ نَفْسِي[218]

O Allah! Inspire in me right guidance, and protect me from the evil of myself [5].

This dua is very important in constant struggle of the person on the path of Allah سبحانه وتعالى. As we learn from our mistakes, our goal is to minimize them especially when and if they displease Allah سبحانه وتعالى. In this regard, asking Allah سبحانه وتعالى for the level of 'rushd' is critical. At this level, a person can have a clear stance of what is right and wrong. This person can make easy and correct decisions that are pleasing to Allah سبحانه وتعالى with Fadl and Rahmah of Allah سبحانه وتعالى. Yet, one's nafs can still constantly work against themselves for the destruction and evil of the person as mentioned with 'wa a'izni min sharri nafsi[219]'.

Most of the time our wrong decisions cause us to be in a state of agitation, uneasiness and fear. The level of 'rushd[220]; includes maturity, wisdom, patience and decision making pleasing to Allah سبحانه وتعالى. Therefore, in terminology, the Khulafau Rashidun[221] known as the guided khalifah (caliphates), are mostly referred to as the four sahabahs[222] who ruled immediately after the Prophet ﷺ passed away. One can see a clear example of 'rushd[223]' embodied in them. One can also see the same level of 'rushd' in some of the elect awliya[224] of Allah سبحانه وتعالى in their stance about issues or problems that can be very difficult for us to make a decision about or to take a position.

---

218. Allahumma alhimni rushdi wa ai'zni min sharri nafsi.
219. *Protect me from the evil of myself.*
220. Spiritual Maturity.
221. Guided caliphs after the demise of the Prophet (saw).
222. The disciples of the Prophet Muhammad who spent time with the Prophet in his lifetime.
223. Spiritual Maturity.
224. The people who are progressing in spiritual journeys and seeking constantly the pleasure of Allah.

Therefore, it is highly suggested to follow a teacher in spiritual and legal matters of the religion if we have difficulty attaining the level of rushd. It is a sign of intelligence when one follows the people of these level as the Quran mentions فَاسْأَلُواْ أَهْلَ الذِّكْرِ إِن كُنتُمْ لاَ تَعْلَمُونَ [225]{43/النحل}. The beginning of this ayah can allude that the people of rushd or 'ahlu dhikr' (people of remembrance) are guided due to the Fadl and Rahmah of Allah سبحانه وتعالى as mentioned وَمَا أَرْسَلْنَا مِن قَبْلِكَ إِلاَّ رِجَالاً نُّوحِي إِلَيْهِمْ, Allahu A'lam.

61. اَللَّهُمَّ إِنِّي أَعُوذُ بِكَ مِنْ زَوَالِ نِعْمَتِكَ وَتَحَوُّلِ عَافِيَتِكَ وَفَجْأَةِ نِقْمَتِكَ وَجَمِيعِ سَخَطِكَ يَا رَحْمٰنُ يَا رَحِيمُ يَا ذَا الْجَلَالِ وَالْإِكْرَامِ يَا حَيُّ يَا قَيُّومُ[226]

O Allah! I seek Your refuge from a cessation of Your grace, the removal of Your protection, a sudden disaster, or any of Your Displeasure. O All-Merciful One! O All-Compassionate One! O Possessor of Majesty and Bounty! O All-Living One! O Self-Subsistent One! [4]

The biggest nimah is iman and everything on this path of struggle of iman, tawhid[227], and ridah[228]. In this regard, any loss that is going to stop, decelerate, and decrease the struggle towards the true iman is considered the loss of nimah. On the contrary, if something is helping to increase and accelerate the quantity and quality of iman then this is nimah.

In this regard, health can be the biggest nimah to achieve this goal. Then, a good company, spouse, and family encouraging to reach this goal can be another nimah. Then, not being distracted or worried about the worldly needs of sustenance, food, shelter, and taking care of others can be another nimah.

225. So ask the people of the dhikr if you do not know, (Nahl:43).
226. Allahumma inni a'uzu bika min zawali ni'matik, wa tahawwuli a'fiyatika, wa fajati niqmatik, wa jamii sakhatika, ya Rahmanu, Ya Rahimu, Ya Zaljalali wa ikrami ya Hayy, Ya Qayyum.
227. Creed system of Oneness & Uniqueness of Allah.
228. Pleasure.

Because, iman requires focus. La ilaha illa Allah[229] requires that the person detaches from everything but focus on one's heart and mind to One, Unique Creator, Allah سبحانه وتعالى with gratitude, humbleness and tawakkul.

The rest of the dua explains what was mentioned above as 'afiyah[230]' which is the physical and mental state of the worry-free person other than this person's focus being only on his or her iman.

As a test, trial or as a consequence of a sin or evil of the person, this person can have niqmah[231] or sakhat[232] of Allah سبحانه وتعالى, may Allah سبحانه وتعالى protect us. It is important to beg and ask Allah سبحانه وتعالى for the avoidance of all the niqmahs and sakhats. When asking from Allah سبحانه وتعالى, we should use the critical names or passcodes such as Ar-Rahman, Ar-Rahim, Zal-Jalali Walikram, Al-Hayy and –Al-Qayyum. They can possibly be Ismu Azam[233] where the duas are accepted when the person calls Allah سبحانه وتعالى with these Names.

229. Can be translated as "there is no deity or god except Allah." This is the creed of Islam called shahadah. Whoever believes in this, is considered Muslim even though the person may not proclaim his or her faith in public, because belief is between the individual and Allah in Islam.
230. Spiritual and bodily well-being.
231. *Disaster.*
232. Displeasure.
233. Greatest Names of Allah (SWT).

62. اَللَّهُمَّ أَحْيِنِي مَا كَانَتِ الْحَيَاةُ خَيْرًا لِي وَتَوَفَّنِي إِذَا كَانَتِ الْوَفَاةُ خَيْرًا لِي[234]

O Allah! Keep me alive as long as life is better for me, and take my soul when death would be better for me! [3]

This is a dua to normalize death in one perspective. It is important to realize and actualize that we are alive now but soon we will die. In this regard, a person is expected to be eager to meet with Allah سبحانه وتعالى. In this sense, this world can be a prison for the person [4] and all the pains, rude and lying engagements can hurt the person in this world. Therefore, the person can be eager to meet with Allah سبحانه وتعالى.

Yet, the person leaves that decision, time and execution to Allah سبحانه وتعالى. Only Allah سبحانه وتعالى knows when or how that would be khair for us and Allah سبحانه وتعالى knows the best. Accordingly, asking Allah سبحانه وتعالى for the best way of living in this world and a way that is pleasing to Allah سبحانه وتعالى are critical. When the person has possibilities of displeasing Allah سبحانه وتعالى, then Allah سبحانه وتعالى knows the best if it is khayr for him to meet with Allah سبحانه وتعالى before this person engages with things displeasing Allah سبحانه وتعالى. Making this type of dua sets the guidelines.

234. Allahumma ahyini ma kaanati alhayatu khayran li wa tawaffni iza kaanati al-wafatu khayran li.

Gratitude and Thankfulness—Hamd and Shukr

63. رَضِينَا بِاللهِ رَبّاً وَبِالْإِسلَامِ دِيناً وَبِمُحَمَّدٍ رَسُولًا، رَضِيتُ بِاللهِ رَبّاً وَبِالْإِسْلَامِ دِينًا وَبِمُحَمَّدٍ نَبِيًّا[235] (٣)

We are content with Allah as our Lord, with Islam as our religion and with Muhammad as our Messenger. I am content with Allah as my Lord, with Islam as my religion, and with Muhammad as my Prophet. (three times) [3]

Sometimes, we don't value what we already have. Recognizing Allah سبحانه وتعالى as our one and only Rabb and being pleased with that is very critical. Then, recognizing the all the teachings that Allah سبحانه وتعالى send us through Islam is another critical point. Then, recognizing the Prophet ﷺ with all his teachings and his status next to Allah as being our leader, guide, teacher and Prophet ﷺ is an inexpressible bounty from Allah سبحانه وتعالى. When we take things for granted, and don't recognize them, then we don't appreciate them even though we have them. Therefore, one of the amazing dispositions the new Muslims have compared to those who were born in Muslims families is that they have the opportunity to compare their life with Islam to their life before accepting the truth. One can also say that one of the wisdoms of evil-looking incidents, or sufferings, is to remind the person this recognition and to encourage the person for recognition and appreciation. Therefore, Allah سبحانه وتعالى reminds us in the Quran with 'Wa la in shakrartum la a'zidannakum[236]'. In other words, the person recognize and still appreciates Rabbul 'Alamin even when facing an evil-seeming incident or a suffering. Therefore, this dua is a very critical reminder that one should say three times in the morning and at night and to really embody the meanings of it.

---

235. Radina billahi rabba wa bil islami dina wa bi Muhammadan rasulan wa nabiyya.

236. {رَبُّكُمْ لَئِن شَكَرْتُمْ لَأَزِيدَنَّكُمْ وَلَئِن كَفَرْتُمْ إِنَّ عَذَابِي لَشَدِيدٌ {إبراهيم/7} (If you are grateful, I will surely increase you [in favor]) (Ibrahim:7).

64. {24/الإسراء} رَّبِّ ارْحَمْهُمَا كَمَا رَبَّيَانِي صَغِيرًا[237]

"O my Sustainer! Bestow Thy grace upon them, even as they cherished and reared me when I was a child!" [1]

Allah سبحانه وتعالى teaches us the etiquettes on how to make dua. In this case, the teaching is about how to make dua to Allah سبحانه وتعالى about one's parents as رَّبِّ ارْحَمْهُمَا كَمَا رَبَّيَانِي صَغِيرًا. In my experience with different Muslim communities, I witnessed the Muslims from Bangladesh frequently making this dua, MashAllah which is an example of the teaching of the Quran being accepted and practiced by the public masses. Unfortunately, it is not the case for all the teachings of the Quran and Sunnah but yet one becomes happy when witnesses at least some of these teachings being implemented.

This dua رَّبِّ ارْحَمْهُمَا كَمَا رَبَّيَانِي صَغِيرًا is very interesting in its chosen words and very correlative and meaningful in the relationship between the parent and child(ren). The relationship between the parent and child(ren) is a cyclic relationship. One can become either a parent, or a child, or both. Experiential knowledge and relevance of this dua is for everyone without any exceptions.

237. Rabbi arhuma kama rabbayani saghiran.

65. اَلْحَمْدُ للهِ الَّذِي أَذْهَبَ عَنِّي الْأَذٰى وَ عَافَانِي[238]

Praise be to Allah Who has ridded me of its harm and kept me healthy [9].

This is a reminder for us that bodily discharge and relief is a very important nimah and blessing from Allah سبحانه وتعالى. One can review the number of diseases in medicine related with issues due to the problems of discharge of the body from its remnants, unused, unnecessary and harmful wastes. One can also review the number of specialties and sub-specialties developed associated with improper bodily discharges. Lastly, one can review the available medicines related with these types of diseases produced by pharmaceutical companies in the market.

On the other hand, a person who realizes this as a nimah and says alhamdulillah after each time he or she uses the restroom can get a reward from Allah سبحانه وتعالى as if this person was worshipping.

The attitude of gratitude is the main theme in Islam with one's relationship with Allah سبحانه وتعالى and then accordingly with others. The first step to gratitude is to realize then verbalize it as mentioned in the Quran and the Sunnah and then lastly act upon it.

Then, the person can revive these feelings of thankfulness by reciting this dua. After making istighfar (seeking forgiveness) and hamd (sending Praise) to Allah سبحانه وتعالى, then the person can read the Prophetic, masnun[239], duas to get back their good health. Then, the person can get medical help, knowing that the medicine is only means and that Allah سبحانه وتعالى can send shifa (healing) with or without them.

238. Alhamdu lillahi allazi azhaba anni alazaa wa a'faani.
239. Prophetic, Sunnah.

There are a lot of duas of the Prophet ﷺ that start with 'hamd'. In these cases, when one analyzes these duas, the first portion shows thankfulness and gratitude to Allah سبحانه وتعالى with the phrase 'Alhamdulillah' (all praise is due to Allah). The second part or expression explains the reason for this gratitude. The third and overall gist of these duas show that gratitude, praise, recognition, and credit should be given to Allah سبحانه وتعالى. In other words, the person does not take any credit for this achievement even if it can be something that seems ordinary like relieving oneself in a bathroom. Because, if the person claims any ownership then, there can be the possibility of shirk (associating partners with Allah سبحانه وتعالى) in one's relationship with Allah سبحانه وتعالى. This can be considered similar to a urine in a pure milk. As one cannot drink this milk even it is a tiny drop, this is similar to the milk representing the purity of iman mixed with the urine of shirk even though it can be an atom size.

With this explanation for example, the above dua starts with thanks and gratitude as Alhamdulillahi[240].

The second and remaining portion explains the reason of this hamd as 'allazi azhaba a'nni a'laza wa a'faani[241].'

Each dua contains this constant notion of giving all due and credit to Allah سبحانه وتعالى for all these nimahs but yet, at the same time denying the portion of the nafs (lowly ego) is critical because the nafs always tries to seek, sneak and steal a portion of due or credit from it. The nafs always wants to be recognized, become famous, and get a position. One can nullify the false and lying approach of the nafs by constantly denying these false claims coming through emotions, feelings and thoughts with the phrase 'astagfirullah' (I seek refuge in Allah). In addition, reading the masnun[242] duas,

240. All gratitude, thanks, appreciation truly belongs to Allah and fully credited to Allah.

241. Who has ridded me of its harm and kept me healthy.

242. Prophetic.

which in their essence, establishes this true iman and belief in Allah سبحانه وتعالى without shirk. In this perspective, the pronouns "I" denoted here in the words a'nni and a'fani can show this process of self-denial.

One should realize that the essence of all these duas is so that the person can embody a true position in their relationship with the Creator, Allah سبحانه وتعالى. In other words, Allah سبحانه وتعالى does not need our gratitude, thanking or glorifying with the phrases Alhamdullilah, SubhanAllah or Allahu Akbar. This is mentioned in various parts of the Quran. For example:

> وَللهِ مَا فِي السَّمَاوَاتِ وَمَا فِي الأَرْضِ وَلَقَدْ وَصَّيْنَا الَّذِينَ أُوتُواْ الْكِتَابَ مِن قَبْلِكُمْ وَإِيَّاكُمْ أَنِ اتَّقُواْ اللّهَ وَإِن تَكْفُرُواْ فَإِنَّ للهِ مَا فِي السَّمَاوَاتِ وَمَا فِي الأَرْضِ وَكَانَ اللّهُ غَنِيًّا حَمِيدًا {النساء/131} وَللهِ مَا فِي السَّمَاوَاتِ وَمَا فِي الأَرْضِ وَكَفَى بِاللهِ وَكِيلاً {النساء/132}

Inversely, we don't know how our position should be with our Creator, Allah سبحانه وتعالى. Therefore, Allah سبحانه وتعالى with the Fadl and Rahmah teaches us through the Prophet ﷺ how this ideal relationship should be embodied and strived in our life long experience.

One can see a similar approach in the duas related with wearing a new dress, someone seeing something liked or disliked. In all cases, hamd to Allah سبحانه وتعالى, giving the due to Allah سبحانه وتعالى but not to oneself, nafs or one's own self.

66. اَلْحَمْدُ للهِ الَّذِي بَعَثَنِي سَالِماً سَوِيًّا[243]

Praise be to Allah, Who awoke me sound and healthy!

Most of the time, we wake up from our sleep feeling well rested. Yet, we don't understand the nimah of waking up healthy and with positive feelings of comfort.

Sometimes, we wake up having a headache, stomach pain and other possible problems. It is expected from a person of iman to not immediately rush to the medical means of feeling better (medicine) but to do a self-reflection. One can remind his or her inner self, nafs, that most of their days can be missing this attitude of gratitude and thankfulness to Allah سبحانه وتعالى by not reciting this dua.

67. اَللَّهُمَّ لَكَ الْحَمْدُ أَنْتَ قَيُّومُ السَّمٰوَاتِ وَالْأَرْضِ وَمَنْ فِيهِنَّ، وَلَكَ الْحَمْدُ أَنْتَ مَلِكُ السَّمٰوَاتِ وَالْأَرْضِ وَمَنْ فِيهِنَّ، وَلَكَ الْحَمْدُ أَنْتَ نُورُ السَّمٰوَاتِ وَالْأَرْضِ وَمَنْ فِيهِنَّ، وَلَكَ الْحَمْدُ أَنْتَ الْحَقُّ وَوَعْدُكَ الْحَقُّ وَلِقَاءُكَ حَقٌّ وَقَوْلُكَ حَقٌّ وَالْجَنَّةُ حَقٌّ وَالنَّارُ حَقٌّ وَالنَّبِيُّونَ حَقٌّ وَمُحَمَّدٌ ﷺ حَقٌّ وَالسَّاعَةُ حَقٌّ. اَللَّهُمَّ لَكَ أَسْلَمْتُ وَبِكَ اٰمَنْتُ وَعَلَيْكَ تَوَكَّلْتُ وَإِلَيْكَ أَنَبْتُ وَبِكَ خَاصَمْتُ وَإِلَيْكَ حَاكَمْتُ فَاغْفِرْ لِي مَا قَدَّمْتُ وَمَآ أَخَّرْتُ وَمَآ أَسْرَرْتُ وَمَآ أَعْلَنْتُ وَمَا أَنْتَ أَعْلَمُ بِهِ مِنِّي. أَنْتَ الْمُقَدِّمُ وَأَنْتَ الْمُؤَخِّرُ لَا إِلٰهَ إِلَّا أَنْتَ وَلاَ حَوْلَ وَلاَ قُوَّةَ إِلاَّ بِاللهِ[244]

O Allah! To You is due all praise for You are the Sustainer of the heavens and the earth and all that is within them. All praise is Yours, for You are the King of the heavens and the earth and

243. Alhamdulillahi Allazi b'athani saliman sawiyya.
244. Allahumma laka hamd Antal Qayyumu Assamawati wal ardi wa man fihinna, wa lakal hamd, Anta Maliku Assamawati wal ardi wa man fihinna, wa lakal hamd, Anta Nuuru Assamawati wal ardi wa man fihinna, wa lakal hamd, Antal Haqq, wa wa'daka haqq, likauka haqq, Qaqluka haqq, aljannatu haqq, annaru haqq, annabiyyu haqq, assa'atu Haqq. Allahumma laka aslamtu wa bika amantu, wa a'layku tawakkaltu, wa ilayka anabtu, wa bika khasamtu, wa ilayka anabtu, wa bika khasamtu, wa ilayka hakamtu, faghfirli ma qadammtu, wa ma akhartu, wa ma asrartu, wa ma a'lantu, wa ma anta a'lamu bihi minni. Antal muqaddimu, wa Antal muakhirru La ilaha illa anta, wa la hawla, wa la quwwata illa billah.

all that is within them. All praise is Yours, for You are the Light of the heavens and the earth and all that is within them. All praise is Yours, for You are the Truth, Your promise is true, the meeting with You is true and Your word is true. Paradise is true, the Hellfire is true, the Prophets are true, Muhammad (peace and blessings be upon him) is true, and the Last Hour is true. O Allah! To You I have submitted, in You do I believe, in You have I put my trust, and unto You I turn in repentance. For Your sake I have disputed, and from You I seek judgment, so forgive me for what I have done and for what I will do, for what I have concealed and what I have declared, and for that [in me] that You know best about. You are the Hastener and the Postponer, there is no god but You, and there is no strength or power except in Allah [14].

Tahaajjud is a special time that Allah سبحانه وتعالى showers humans with a special Tajalli. Especially at the last third portion of the night, this tajalli is very unique as mentioned by Rasulullah [3] ﷺ 4]].

If one analyzes the wordings of this dua, the da'i (caller) uses the 'muhattab' prononun "ta" or "ka" with the words "Laka and Anta" as if the person is in front of Rabbul Alamin, talking to Allah سبحانه وتعالى.

In addition, the word "al-haqq" is used to indicate, this certainty in different parts of iman.

For example:

Antal Haqq: *You are the Truth*
Wa Wa'daka Haqq: *Your promise is true,*
Liqaika Haqq: *the meeting with You is true*
Qawluka Haqq: *Your word is true*
Aljannatu Haqq: The *Heaven is true*

Annaru Haqq: *The Hellfire is true*

Annabiyyu Haqq: *The Prophets are true*

Muhammadun Haqq: *Muhammad (peace and blessings be upon him) is true*

Assa'atu Haqq: *The Last Hour is true*

In other words, if one wants to reach the level of 'yaqin', certainty in their iman, then this can be achieved with regular prayers of tahajjud.

Then, the levels of Islam (aslamtu), Iman[245] (amantu), Tawakkul[246] (tawakkultu), Inabah[247] (Anabtu) happen and proceed as these wordings are mentioned in this dua.

In all these engagements of one's effort of being closer to Allah سبحانه وتعالى, there is either an increase with the Fadl and Rahmah of Allah سبحانه وتعالى as mentioned Antal Muqaddimu[248]. Or, if the person does not care, and chooses not to engage, then the possibility of degrading can happen as mentioned al-muakhirru[249].

So, tahajjud entails all these possibilities. Therefore, the dua starts with Hamd for Allah سبحانه وتعالى for any good engagement and nimah. The dua ends to remind oneself all these good engagements are with the Fadl, Rahmah, Hawl and Quwwah of Allah سبحانه وتعالى but not from the person as mentioned in 'La hawla wa la quwwata illa billah' (There is no strength, enablement, and power except with the enablement, by Allah سبحانه وتعالى).

Allahu A'lam.

Allahumma Ja'alna minal mutahajjiduun[250], Amin.

245. Belief.
246. Reliance.
247. Return.
248. *The Hastener.*
249. *The Postponer.*
250. Oh Allah! Make us from the ones who pray to you at night, amen.

Traveling and Fear—Safar

68. اَللّٰهُمَّ إِنِّي أَعُوذُ بِكَ مِنْ وَعْثَاءِ السَّفَرِ وَكَآبَةِ الْمَنْظَرِ وَسُوءِ الْمُنْقَلَبِ فِي الْمَالِ وَ الأَهْلِ وَالْوَلَدِ[251]

O Allah, I seek refuge in You from the hardships of travelling, unhappiness connected with ghastly scenes and evil turns into our property, family, and children. [4]

Anything can happen to a person at any time. When a person is traveling, the probability of undesired incidents and calamities can increase due to the unknowns. Unknowns of the road, unknowns of different strangers, unavailability of help, and psychological distress can all make this traveling engagement very painful and scary. Therefore, making this dua is critical each time to remember and seek refuge in Allah سبحانه وتعالى from all these unknown and possible calamities. Allah سبحانه وتعالى is al-Hayy[252], al-Hafiz[253], al-Rahim[254] and al-Basir[255]. When the person has these concerns, then Allah سبحانه وتعالى is going to protect the person inshAllah. But, when the person doesn't remember this and just sees traveling as fun, then this person can attract all these possible problems.

Therefore, in these most expected weak moments, the ayahs in the Quran depicts the people while traveling in the sea with these all unknowns so that the person can realize his or her real weak disposition. Ayahs mention that in these instances the people are forced to be reminded of their weakness.

---

251. Allahumma inni a'udhu bika min wa'tha'is-safari, wa kaabatil-manzari, wa su'il-munqalabi fil-mali wal-ahli wal-waladi.
252. All Alive and All Active.
253. The Protector.
254. The Merciful.
255. All Watcher.

For example: قُلْ مَن يُنَجِّيكُم مِّن ظُلُمَاتِ الْبَرِّ وَالْبَحْرِ تَدْعُونَهُ تَضَرُّعاً وَخُفْيَةً لَّئِنْ أَنجَانَا مِنْ هَذِهِ لَنَكُونَنَّ مِنَ الشَّاكِرِينَ {الأنعام/٦٣} قُلِ اللّهُ يُنَجِّيكُم مِّنْهَا وَمِن كُلِّ كَرْبٍ ثُمَّ أَنتُمْ تُشْرِكُونَ {الأنعام/64} *"Say, "Who rescues you from the darknesses of the land and sea [when] you call upon Him imploring [aloud] and privately, 'If He should save us from this [crisis], we will surely be among the thankful. Say, "It is Allah who saves you from it and from every distress; then you [still] associate others with Him."* (An'am:63–64) [1].

> هُوَ الَّذِي يُسَيِّرُكُمْ فِي الْبَرِّ وَالْبَحْرِ حَتَّى إِذَا كُنتُمْ فِي الْفُلْكِ وَجَرَيْنَ بِهِم بِرِيحٍ طَيِّبَةٍ وَفَرِحُواْ بِهَا جَاءتْهَا رِيحٌ عَاصِفٌ وَجَاءهُمُ الْمَوْجُ مِن كُلِّ مَكَانٍ وَظَنُّواْ أَنَّهُمْ أُحِيطَ بِهِمْ دَعَوُاْ اللّهَ مُخْلِصِينَ لَهُ الدِّينَ لَئِنْ أَنجَيْتَنَا مِنْ هَذِهِ لَنَكُونَنِّ مِنَ الشَّاكِرِينَ {يونس/22} فَلَمَّا أَنجَاهُمْ إِذَا هُمْ يَبْغُونَ فِي الأَرْضِ بِغَيْرِ الْحَقِّ يَا أَيُّهَا النَّاسُ إِنَّمَا بَغْيُكُمْ عَلَى أَنفُسِكُم مَّتَاعَ الْحَيَاةِ الدُّنْيَا ثُمَّ إِلَينَا مَرْجِعُكُمْ فَنُنَبِّئُكُم بِمَا كُنتُمْ تَعْمَلُونَ {يونس/23}
>
> *"It is He who enables you to travel on land and sea until, when you are in ships and they sail with them by a good wind and they rejoice therein, there comes a storm wind and the waves come upon them from everywhere and they assume that they are surrounded [i.e., doomed], supplicating Allah, sincere to Him in religion, "If You should save us from this, we will surely be among the thankful. But when He saves them, at once they commit injustice upon the earth without right. O mankind, your injustice is only against yourselves, [being merely] the enjoyment of worldly life. Then to Us is your return, and We will inform you of what you used to do."* (Yunus:22–23) [1].

Yet later, some forget and some change. May Allah سبحانه وتعالى protect us. Amin.

When the person is traveling, there is always the possibility of changing conditions as the person is not in his or her most comfortable setting. In other words, the real purpose of life is to embody the dhikr of La ilaha illa Allah. A person gains real happiness when the person focuses his or her heart and life on Allah سبحانه وتعالى. Normally, this focusing is difficult due to different distractions, responsibilities and engagements of life. Traveling adds more distractions, and distress on one's spiritual mood. Therefore, a person can lose one's spiritual balance during traveling if there is no proper patience. It has been suggested that one of the ways to know the true stamina and character of a person is to travel with him or her.

Full Submission—Islam

69. لَبَّيْكَ اللهُمَّ لَبَّيْكَ، لَبَّيْكَ لَا شَرِيكَ لَكَ لَبَّيْكَ، إِنَّ الْحَمْدَ وَالنِّعْمَةَ لَكَ وَالْمُلْكَ، لَا شَرِيكَ لَكَ[256]

At Your beckoning and call, O Allah! At Your service! At Your service! No partner You have! At Your service! Truly praise and grace are Yours, and the dominion; no partner have You [3].

The expression Labbayk[257] can denote the full attitude of submission to Allah. In colloquial Arabic one can say "khãdir!" or tahta amrika as Egyptians say which can mean "I am under your order or under your command." Yet, this is repeated thrice as Labbayk, Allahumma Labbayk[258] with emphasis and then Labbayk comes again. Then, the real core and the essence comes when the person submits him or herself. The person is choosing not to take any partners or associates in one's relationship with Allah سبحانه وتعالى as mentioned 'la sharika laka'[259]. If one analyzes the faridah or requirement of Hajj or umra, it is really a level of maturity as a ritual when one performs it. In this ritual there are requirements and conditions such as money, health and other means. In its time requirement, for example, Hajj is only possible once a year and even for just a few specific days in a month. According to many scholars of Fiqh, hajj is even just during the period of time being in arafah[260]. Meaning that catching that time at that place of arafah is the only required part of Hajj and others come with less requirements. So, it is expected and observed that when the person decides to perform this ritual, the person already had some portion of exercise from other required rituals of Islam. For example, when there is a firework show, the last or

---

256. Labbayk Allahumma Labbayk, Labbayk La Sharika Laka Labbayk, Innal Hamda, wa ni'mata Laka, wal mulka, La Sharika Laka.
257. *At Your service!*
258. *At Your beckoning and call, O Allah! At Your service!*
259. *No partner You have!*
260. The name of a hill in Maccah.

final performance can be the most amazing one. Similarly, hajj and umrah can require the full embodiment of this notion of 'la sharika laka[261]' in its different rituals.

In this dua, dhikr or chant, something is reminding the person that although we thank to people, the real thanks, gratitude, in their full and perfect quantity and quality belongs to Allah سبحانه وتعالى as mentioned in 'Innal Hamda Laka[262]'. Similarly, the expressions 'wa ni'mata Laka' and 'wal mulka Laka[263]' reminds the person that the Real Owner and the Real Giver is Allah سبحانه وتعالى. So don't make shirk as the chant ends with again la sharika laka.

---

261. *No partner You have!*
262. *Truly praise and grace are Yours.*
263. *The dominion is Yours.*

70. لَبَّيْكَ، لَبَّيْكَ وَسَعْدَيْكَ وَالْخَيْرُ بِيَدَيْكَ وَالرَّغْبَاءُ إِلَيْكَ وَالْعَمَلُ، لَبَّيْكَ لَبَّيْكَ إِلٰهَ الْحَقِّ لَبَّيْكَ[264]

At Your beckoning and call! At Your service, and Your pleasure! All goodness is in Your hands; the aspiring turn to You, and all works are for You. At Your beckoning and call, God of truth! At Your service! [4]

The main part of the ihram is accepting that one is fully submitting to Allah سبحانه وتعالى as a Muslim with the constant repetition of the expression 'labbayk[265]'. Then, once the person admits and accepts this, the notions of shirk can come especially when the person tries to seek benefit or good from others. In this regard, knowing that the main source of all good and benefit comes from Allah سبحانه وتعالى as mentioned in the expression 'wal khayru biyadayk[266]' can eliminate most of the gaps of shirk, Allahu A'lam.

The expression 'wa ra'ghbau ilayka[267]' can show that in all the cases of problems, good, evil, family issues, family and friend positive bonds, the person needs to desire to constantly turn to Allah سبحانه وتعالى. In this regard, what happens should not really deeply affect the person. They can have some effect as a human such as happiness, sadness, broken hearts, joy and other alternative feelings and emotions. Yet, the person's real asset is iman, the relationship with Allah سبحانه وتعالى.

For example, the person's spouse hurts the person, then the person goes back to Allah سبحانه وتعالى, cries and restores his or her energy and collects oneself. The person is hurt by his or her children or parents then he does the same, goes back to Allah سبحانه وتعالى, cries and restores his or her energy and collects oneself. The person is

264. Labbayk, labbayk wa sa'dayk, wal khayru biyadayk war raghbau ilayka wal a'malu, labbayk labbayk, ilahal Haq, labbayk.
265. *At Your service, and Your pleasure!*
266. *All goodness is in Your hands.*
267. *The aspiring turn to You.*

so happy and in an extreme state of joy, then the person goes back to Allah سبحانه وتعالى, cries and thanks Allah سبحانه وتعالى for all the bounties he or she does not even deserve. Then, the person can in the natural, neutral and happy state of zuhd by avoiding shirk and by remembering and showing gratitude to Allah سبحانه وتعالى but he or she does not claim any ownership in achieving this good.

One can remember the beginning expression as 'Labbayk wa sa'dayk[268]', the real happiness is going back to Allah سبحانه وتعالى by pleasing Allah سبحانه وتعالى and but not with anything else. This is very important as we constantly forget.

The part 'wa'amalu' can signify that all the actions in their essence should be for Allah سبحانه وتعالى but no one else. We sometimes engage ourselves with different things to please others. Therefore, in both legal rulings and in the teachings of tasawwuf or the teachings of ahlul qalb (the people of heart), the intention before each action is the key. The person needs to focus and ask him or herself what is one's intention. Then, if it is not for Allah سبحانه وتعالى, then the person must re-evaluate doing this action by either avoiding it or doing this action with an intention and a manner that is pleasing to Allah سبحانه وتعالى.

268. At *Your pleasure!*

71. لَا إِلَهَ إِلَّا اللهُ وَحْدَهُ أَنْجَزَ وَعْدَهُ وَنَصَرَ عَبْدَهُ وَهَزَمَ الْأَحْزَابَ وَحْدَهُ، لَا إِلَهَ إِلَّا اللهُ وَلَا نَعْبُدُ إِلَّا إِيَّاهُ مُخْلِصِينَ لَهُ الدِّينَ وَلَوْ كَرِهَ الْكَافِرُونَ[269]

There is no god but Allah who has fulfilled the Divine promise, supported the seeker, worshipper, and adorer of Allah, and Who alone defeated the troops. There is no god but Allah, and we don't worship anything but Allah, devoting ourselves in religion entirely to Allah, despite the dislike of ungrateful ones and disbelievers [3].

One of the most important parts of hajj is the embodiment of tawhid (oneness of Allah). Tawhid requires one to embody 'La ilaha illa Allah[270]' with all its faculties. We think that we embody these faculties but in its essence we may have a lot of problems, and black holes. To repair these holes, 'wahdahu[271]' imbibes the person to instill oneness of Allah سبحانه وتعالى.

'Wa nasara a'bdahu[272]' shows the person that Allah سبحانه وتعالى is the One Who really enables and gives the person the means to do good. The results of the achievements and the due should all be given to Allah سبحانه وتعالى as mentioned 'wa hazama al-ahzaaba wahdahu[273]'. Then, in all this engagements, one should remember the key phrase of La ilaha illa Allah.

Then, in all explicit or implicit forms of worship we turn to Allah سبحانه وتعالى, 'wa la na'budu illa iyyahu[274]'. These in all their essence can be called ikhlas (sincerity). Therefore, we fully turn

269. La ilaha illa Allahu wahdahu anjaza wa'dahu, wa nasara a'bdahu, wa hazamal ahzaaba wahdahu, la ilaha illa Allah, wa la na'budu illa iyyahu, mukhlisiina lahu addiina wa law karihal kafiruun.
270. "there is no deity or god except Allah."
271. *Alone.*
272. *Supported His servant.*
273. *Who alone defeated the troops.*
274. *We don't worship anything but Him.*

to Allah سبحانه وتعالى in the matters of the religion as mentioned 'mukhlisiina lahu addina[275]'.

Yet, when one looks at the kafir (disbeliever), it's obvious that they don't care that they are committing shirk and kufr. And even, they don't like that we fully turn to Allah سبحانه وتعالى without making any shirk and associations with Allah سبحانه وتعالى. If that is the case, don't worry about them and move on with ikhlas to establish true tawhid in your relationship with Allah سبحانه وتعالى.

When a person wins a victory, that person may feel accomplished or give credit to their self for this achievement. In the expression 'wa hazama al-ahzaaba wahdahu[276]", the word 'wahdahu' indicated that no due should be given to the person. All the good and achievements are given by Allah سبحانه وتعالى and with the Fadl (favor), and Rahmah (mercy) of Allah سبحانه وتعالى. This is one of the critical and dangerous points people lose when they seem to win or achieve victory. Because sometimes it is more difficult to maintain one's inner self of being with Allah سبحانه وتعالى with humbleness when a person is given a ni'mah (blessing). Therefore, a true n'imah does not make the person arrogant but make the person more humble, appreciative and grateful to Allah سبحانه وتعالى. This can be a means of measure if something is a nimah or istidraj[277].

---

275. *Devoting ourselves in religion entirely to Him.*
276. *Who alone defeated the troops.*
277. Test.

72. اَللَّهُمَّ مَا صَلَّيْتُ مِنْ صَلَاةٍ فَعَلٰى مَنْ صَلَّيْتَ وَمَا لَعَنْتُ مِنْ لَعْنٍ فَعَلٰى مَنْ لَعَنْتَ إِنَّكَ وَلِيِّي فِي الدُّنْيَا وَلْاٰخِرَةِ تَوَفَّنِي مُسْلِماً وَأَلْحِقْنِي بِالصَّالِحِينَ[278]

O Allah! Let whomsoever I have invoked blessings on, be those whom You have blessed, and whomsoever I invoked curses on, be those whom You have cursed. Verily You are my protector in this life and in the Hereafter, so take my soul as a Muslim and join me with the righteous [10].

At the end, what matters is that what and how Allah سبحانه وتعالى wants or doesn't want something. The word salla establishes a connection with the things and items what and how Allah سبحانه وتعالى is pleased with. One can call this the guidelines of halal. On the other hand, the word la'nta explains about the things and items that Allah سبحانه وتعالى is displeased with. This can be called the harams. At the end, we don't invent or discover them, it is already established. In a lifespan, the person with certainty can understand why and how these are made halal or haram. Yet, the person is expected to follow them not because it makes sense but due to the person's disposition of submission to Allah سبحانه وتعالى. This disposition and innate character and trait is mentioned with the phrase as "Musliman." Everyone in their initial state of birth as a baby is in this state of weakness, and full submission. Therefore, in the journey of life, one should not lose this attitude embedded as the true disposition of the nafs, self by being engaged with the lies of arrogance as the person grows up, becomes physically strong, and intellectually advanced. Therefore, meeting Allah سبحانه وتعالى with the initial state of humbleness and submission is imperative and vital. The expression "tawaffani Musliman[279]" is teaching us to ask Allah سبحانه وتعالى for this necessary final state at the verge of death.

---

278. Allahumma ma salaytu min salatin faa'la man salayta wa ma la'nta min la'nin fa'la man la'nta, innaka waliyyi fid dunya wal akhirati tawaffani Musliman, wa alhiqni bis salihiin.
279. *Take my soul as a Muslim.*

Achievements of the Day—Khayr

73. رَبِّ إِنِّي أَسْأَلُكَ خَيْرَ مَا فِي هٰذَا الْيَوْمِ وَخَيْرَ مَا بَعْدَهُ وَأَعُوذُ بِكَ مِنْ شَرِّ مَا فِي
هٰذَا الْيَوْمِ وَشَرِّ مَا بَعْدَهُ[280]

O Lord! I ask You for the goodness of this day, and the goodness of the days thereafter and I seek refuge in You from the evil of this day and the evil thereafter. O Lord! I take refuge in You from sloth and troubles of old age [8].

Every day is a challenge. Anything can happen at any time. This dua removes the burden from the weak shoulders of the person. This dua makes the person fully submit him or herself to Allah سبحانه وتعالى. This dua brings security, calmness and ease on the heart and mind. This dua further tells the person to ask from Allah سبحانه وتعالى the best, the openings, the victories, the triumphs, the guidance, and the lights of this day. As well as, it is important ask protection from all evil that can come to the person on this day, may Allah سبحانه وتعالى protect us in all of our days, and gives us openings and victories of guidance and iman with afiyah and ease, amin.

280. Rabbi inni asalaku khayra ma fi haza al yawmi wa khayra ma ba'dahu wa au'zu bika min sharri ma fi hazal yawmi wa sharri ma ba'dahu.

74. اَللّٰهُمَّ اجْعَلْنِي صَبُورًا وَاجْعَلْنِي شَكُورًا وَاجْعَلْنِي فِي عَيْنِي صَغِيرًا وَفِي أَعْيُنِ النَّاسِ كَبِيرًا[281]

O Allah! Make me [constantly] patient, and make me ever grateful! Make me insignificant in my own eyes, but great in the eyes of people!

A person may not understand and embody the meaning of this dua initially. Because, a genuine person who is worshipping to Allah سبحانه وتعالى does not care about what others think. He or she always see him or herself as the lowest of the low. This is the reality of a human if he or she wants to excel.

The feelings of being something, having arrogance or pride, considering that world is evolving around this person and other similar feelings are lies, distractions, disgusting dishonesties and deceits constantly instilled by one's own nafs and shaytan. This the reality about one's own self. This is not humbleness or humility but reality.

On the other hand, as humans are in the realm of humans, there are general realities of humans. People give value and accordingly respect power, position, wealth and all these marketing or symbolic tools. In these realities pumped up by shaytan and egos, one can ask to سبحانه وتعالى to be valued or respected for a purpose. This purpose can be due to when one relates the people about the diamond and pearl valued realities of the Quran and Sunnah, so that, people would listen, respect and consider these critical realities, Allahu A'lam. People generally listen, respect and value something if it is coming from an important person. Today's media sector is mostly based on this reality by constantly broadcasting people of fame, good or bad, to increase their rating [19].

281. Allahumma ja'alni sabuuran waja'lni shakuran, waja'lani fi a'yni saghiran wa fi a'yuni annasi kabiiran.

This really has a double sided sword: on one side being internally nothing and on the other side having a dress on you for being someone very important and worth being listened to. If these two are mixed, the person can lose both his or her dunya and akhirah, may Allah سبحانه وتعالى protect us, Amin. Only, the people of higher caliber with Allah SWT can do this. At our time, there may be few or none of these people.

Along with this dua, one should review the hadith of Rasulullah ﷺ [4] about the concept of praise and how it can kill the person. The amanah[282] mentioned in Surah Ahzab[283] that resulted in rejection of the mountains but acceptance of the humans can be related to embodying these two balances being nothing in reality yet, being something virtually or externally, Allahu A'lam. This is very difficult to achieve.

282. Responsibility.
283. Surah Ahzab:72.

Embodiment of Faith—Iman

75. اَللَّهُمَّ اجْعَلْ فِي قَلْبِي نُوراً وَفِي سَمْعِي نُورًا وَفِي بَصَرِي نُورًا[284]

O Allah! Grant me light in my heart, light in my hearing and light in my sight! [3]

As we deal daily, hourly and minutely and even secondly with stresses, anxieties, fears, uneasiness, unknowns, worries, agitations, discomforts, nervousness, restlessness, uncertainties, irritations, pains, and confrontations. Making this dua can put the person's heart (qalb) in tranquility, ease, comfort, rest and calmness. To reach this state of heart, the intake or food of heart should be healthy through the eyes and ears. In other words, for the person to reach this state of heart, what one sees and hears are the determining factors.

One can witness this development in children. When a toddler is surrounded with pure, clean and healthy interactions by hearing the words of iman, the Quran, the hadith, gentleness, love, and seeing and observing pictures and scenes of nature, then one can witness a very nice, calm and sweet child. As soon as the child is exposed to the man-made world of listening and the sounds of vulgar and obscene language and visual and seeing remnants and residues through games, videos, internet or TV related items, then the child becomes agitated with fears and nightmares [20]. One can witness this phenomenon of increasing terror in children at our current times among other terrors linked to these artificial and harmful exposures [21].

Sometimes, some evil or waswasa renderings can come to the person's heart. The person should guard their heart from all these spiritual filth inducing thoughts at all times. The first means of guarding the heart is to ask Allah سبحانه وتعالى for help.

284. Allahumma aja'ln fi qalbi nuuraan, wa fi sam'i nuuran wa fi basari nuran.

The second is to continue one's routine awrad. The third is not give importance to these renderings. The sweetness of iman as mentioned 'Allahumma aja'ln fi qalbi nuuraan[285]' will always put the person in calm and tranquil states. On the other hand, the shaytan's occupation is to break this line of sweetness. May Allah سبحانه وتعالى protect us and not leave us with our own nafs, Amin.

76. اَللَّهُمَّ اجْعَلْنَا نُحِبُّكَ وَنُحِبُّ مَلٰئِكَتَكَ وَأَنْبِيَاءَكَ وَرُسُلَكَ وَنُحِبُّ عِبَادَكَ الصَّالِحِينَ.
اَللَّهُمَّ حَبِّبْنَا إِلَيْكَ وَإِلَى مَلٰئِكَتِكَ وَإِلَى أَنْبِيَائِكَ وَرُسُلِكَ وَإِلَى عِبَادِكَ الصَّالِحِينَ[286]

Oh Allah! Make us love You, and love Your angels, Your prophets, Your messengers, and Your righteous seekers, worshippers, and adorers!

Oh Allah! Endear us to You, and to Your angels, Your prophets, Your messengers, and Your righteous seekers, worshippers, and adorers!"

One can sometimes think about one's goal and purpose in life. As humans are social, it is normal to expect affinity and love among each other. Yet, a person concerned with the worries of akhirah[287] can be tired of humanly interest and selfish based relationships. These relationships are meaningless and temporary and suffering embedded and implanted due to its deadlines and end times. The only way to maintain the relationships without suffering and for them to be meaningful, truly beneficial, full of reward and joy is to connect with the One Who is not ending, not restricted by time, Who can help and benefit in this dunya[288] and Akhirah. The only One is Allah سبحانه وتعالى.

---

285. *O Allah! Grant me light in my heart.*
286. Allahumma aja'lna nuhibbuka wa nuhibbu malaikataka wa anbiyaka wa rasuluka wa nuhibbu I'badaka assalihiin. Allahumma habibna ilayka wa ila malaikatika wa ila anbiyaika wa rasuluka wa ila I'badaka assalihin.
287. Afterlife.
288. Worldly life.

Yes, when one builds all the relationships, kinship, love, affinity, social, friendship, family, professional and all others in somehow attaching to the real relationship with Allah سبحانه وتعالى, then the relationships become not hurtful, not scary, not stressful, and unfearful. But, they become beneficial, meaningful, full of reward and joy, bold and fruitful.

When one analyzes this dua, this is the essence of the dua. First and foremost, the person asks to love Allah سبحانه وتعالى and that Allah سبحانه وتعالى loves this person.

The other groups of the malaika (angels), anbiya (prophets), and salihun (the righteous) all are certified in the relationship of Loved and Beloved. Therefore, their love becomes meaningful for this person as a possible group identity of being with them. As Rasulullah ﷺ mentions that a person is with the one whom he or she loves [4]. Another hadith mentions when Allah سبحانه وتعالى is pleased with a person, Allah calls Angel Jibril and announces to him His love for that person. Then, Angel Jibril[289] announces this among the other malaikah (angels) and all the angels love this person. Then, the angels send love to the earth for this person [4].

Therefore, one should really consider how one should direct one's inclinations, love and affinity accordingly to others, because as humans we are social. We get sad when we don't get attention and love. People around us may then blame us by saying that we don't have friends or seem lonely. Those can all be externally wrong judgments of people. If the person embodies this dua of Rasulullah ﷺ. Then, this person makes the correct investment about the choice of friendship compared to his or her other fellows regardless of how they may view this person, Allahu A'lam.

289. Gabriel.

77. اَللَّهُمَّ مَا قُلْتُ مِنْ قَوْلٍ أَوْ حَلَفْتُ مِنْ حَلِفٍ أَوْ نَذَرْتُ مِنْ نَذْرٍ أَوْ عَمِلْتُ مِنْ عَمَلٍ فَمَشِيئَتُكَ بَيْنَ يَدَيْ ذٰلِكَ كُلُّهُ، مَا شِئْتَ كَانَ وَمَا لَمْ تَشَأْ لَمْ يَكُنْ وَلاَ حَوْلَ وَلاَ قُوَّةَ إِلاَّ بِكَ إِنَّكَ عَلٰى كُلِّ شَيْءٍ قَدِيرٌ[290]

O Allah! Whatever words I have uttered, oaths I have sworn, vows I have made, or deeds I have done, all depends on Your will. Whatever You willed was and whatever You willed not was not. There is no strength or power except in You, and truly You have power over all things [10].

It is important to embody the true understanding that a person can only act with the allowance of Allah سبحانه وتعالى. This may be called destiny. Yet, regardless of the term, knowing this can make the person fully rely on Allah سبحانه وتعالى. This understanding can then protect the person from all fears and anxieties.

78. اَللَّهُمَّ إِنِّي أَسْأَلُكَ الرِّضَا بَعْدَ الْقَضٰى وَبَرْدَ الْعَيْشِ بَعْدَ الْمَوْتِ وَلَذَّةَ النَّظَرِ إِلٰى وَجْهِكَ وَشَوْقاً إِلٰى لِقَائِكَ مِنْ غَيْرِ ضَرَّاءَ مُضِرَّةٍ وَلَا فِتْنَةٍ مُضِلَّةٍ وَأَعُوذُ بِكَ أَنْ أَظْلِمَ أَوْ أُظْلَمَ أَوْ أَعْتَدِيَ أَوْ يُعْتَدٰى عَلَيَّ أَوْ أَكْسِبَ خَطِيئَةً أَوْ ذَنْبًا لَا يُغْفَرُ[291]

O Allah! I ask You for contentment with what You decree, a life of bliss after death, the joy of beholding Your Countenance, and longing for the meeting with You, safe from injury by what is harmful and from any trial that might cause me to go astray. I seek refuge in You from wronging others and being wronged, from committing aggression and being the object of aggression, and from committing an error or committing a sin which is not forgiven [14].

---

290. Allahumma ma qultu min qawlin aw halaftu min halifin, aw nazartu min nazrin, aw a'miltu min a'malin, famashi'tuka bayna yaday, zalika kulluh, ma shi'ta kana wa ma shi'ta lam yakun, wa la hawla wa la quwwata illa bika innaka a'la kulli shayin qadiir.
291. Allahumma inni asaluka Arrida ba'da al-Qada, wa barda a'yshi ba'dal mawti, wa lazzata annazari ila wajhika, wa shawqan ila liqaika min gayri darra a mudirratin wa la fitnatin mudillatin, wa au'zu bika an azlima aw uzlama aw a'tadiya aw yu'tada a'layya aw aksiba khatiiatan aw zanban la yughfaru.

One can know that one of the highest 'lazzah[292]' in afterlife is seeing Allah سبحانه وتعالى. There are sins, may Allah سبحانه وتعالى protect us and forgive us, that may cause the person to lose this nimah of seeing Allah سبحانه وتعالى in the afterlife. The last part of the dua can indicate reaching to these nimahs in ease.

79. اَللَّهُمَّ اِجْعَلْ خَيْرَ عُمْرِي اٰخِرَهُ وَخَيْرَ عَمَلِي خَوَاتِمَهُ وَخَيْرَ أَيَّامِي يَوْمَ أَلْقَاكَ فِيهِ[293]

Make the best part of my life its end, the best of my deeds my final deed, and the best of my days the day I meet with You.

80. اَللَّهُمَّ إِنِّي أَسْأَلُكَ عِيشَةً نَقِيَّةً وَمِيتَةً سَوِيَّةً وَمَرَدًّا غَيْرَ مَخْزى وَلا فَاضِحٍ[294]

O Allah! I ask You to grant me a pure life, a good end and a return in the Hereafter free from dishonor or scandal [16].

In the above duas of the Prophet ﷺ, there is the normalization of the reality of death. Mainly, two questions are the main points of focus: how we do normalize this? how do we set a goal for it?

As we age, we tend to cover or hide our aging emotionally and physically. We don't want to accept it. We tend to oversee it. We tend to hide it. But if one analyzes the hadith and sayings of the Prophet ﷺ, death is a reality and we shouldn't separate it from our daily lives. For example, the statement of the Prophet ﷺ when passing through a qabr[295], he ﷺ speaks to the deceased and says "You left before us, and we will meet you soon, inshAllah." [4] [9] [14]

292. Pleasure.
293. Allahumma ija'l khayr u'muri akhirahu wa khayra a'mali khawatimahu, wa khayra ayyami yawma alqaaka fiih.
294. Allahumma inni asaluka I'shatan naqiyyatan wa mitatan sawiiyatan wa maraddan ghayra makhza wa la faadih.
295. Cemetery

In this case, Rasulullah ﷺ teaches us a very logical engagement with death. He ﷺ asks the last few years, or months, of person to be spent in such a way that it would be most pleasing to Allah سبحانه وتعالى.

For example, when there is the final of a game, or an exam or a fireworks show, the final is expected to weigh more than others. Because, the person can make such a move in the final portion that can change everything.

The following dua furthers the concept of death and includes the portion when the person meets with Allah سبحانه وتعالى. The words mitatan sawiyyatan wa maraddan ghayra makhza wa la fadihin[296]' are important to think about. In one's life, the person can be engaged with different things assuming that they are good but, he or she may not know about it for sure until this person dies and the reality is shown to him. The words 'maraddan ghayra makhza wa la fadihin[297]' can indicate asking and begging to Allah سبحانه وتعالى to avoid this type of disappointment.

296. *A good end and a return in the Hereafter free from dishonor or scandal.*
297. A return in the Hereafter free from dishonor and scandal.

BIBLIOGRAPHY

[1] SInternational, The Quran, Abul-Qasim Publishing House, 1997.

[2] M. Asad, The message of the Quran: Translated and explained., Al-Andalus Gibraltar, 1980.

[3] M. i. I. Bukhārī, UK Islamic Academy, 2005.

[4] A. Muslim, Sahih Muslim (translated by Siddiqui, A.), Peace Vision, 1972.

[5] M. Tirmizi, Jami At-Tirmizi, Dar-us-Salam, 2007.

[6] A. i. A. B. al-Haythami, Majma al-Zawa'id, Beirut: Mu'assash al-Ma'arif, 1986.

[7] M. Razi, Mafatih al-Ghayb known as al-Tafsir al-Kabir, Cairo: Dar Ibya al-Kutub al-Bahiyya, 1172.

[8] S. Abu-Dawud, Sunan Abu Dawud, Riyadh: Darussalam, 2008.

[9] I. Majah, Sunan Ibn-i-Majah, Kitab Bhavan, 2000.

[10] A. B. Hanbal, Musnad Imam Ahmad Ibn Hanbal, Dar-Us-Salam Publications, 2012.

[11] I. Darimi, Sunan Darimi, Beirut: Dar Al Kitab, 1997.

[12] A. al-Bayhaqi, Al-Sunan Al-Kabir, Dar 'Aalim al-Kutub, 2013.

[13] I. Hibban, As-Sahih, Beirut: Dar Ibn Hazm, 2012, pp. 4/612, 6/411.

[14] A. An-Nasa'i, Sunan An-Nasai, Riyadh: Daraussalalm, 2007.

[15] S. Vahide, The Collection of Light, ihlas nur publication, 2001.

[16] M. i. A. Hakim, Al-Mustadrak: `ala al-sahihayn, Dar al-Kutub al-`Ilmiyyah, 1990, p. 1/612.

[17] S. Tabarani, Kitabu Ad-Dua, Darul Hadis, 2014.

[18] A. Tahawi, Sharh Al Kabir A'la Al-Aqeedah Al-TahwawiI, Dar Al-Dhakha'ir, 2017.

[19] S. H. D. B. S. Mark Balnaves, Media Theories and Approaches: A Global Perspective, Macmillan International Higher Education, 2008.
[20] J. Cantor, Mommy, I'm Scared: How TV and Movies Frighten Children and what We Can Do to Protect Them, Harcourt Brace, 1998.
[21] M. McCluskey, News Framing of School Shootings: Journalism and American Social Problems, Lexington Books, 2016.

COMMENTATOR'S BIO

Dr. M. Yunus Kumek is currently teaching on Muslim Ministry and Spiritual Care at Harvard Divinity School. He has been religious studies coordinator at State University of New York (SUNY) Buffalo State and teaching undergraduate and graduate courses in religious studies at SUNY at Buffalo State, Niagara University and Daemen College. Before becoming interested in religious studies, Dr. Kumek was doing his doctorate degree in physics at SUNY at Buffalo, and had published academic papers in the areas of quantum physics and medical physics. Then, he decided to engage with the world of social sciences through social anthropology, education, and cultural anthropology in his doctorate studies and subsequently, spent a few years as a research associate in the anthropology department of the same university. Recently, he completed a postdoctoral fellowship at Harvard Divinity school and published books on religious literacy through ethnography and selected passages from the Quran with interpreted contextual meanings. Dr. Kumek had classical training in Islamic sciences from the teachers of Egypt, India, Turkey, Yemen, Somalia, Morocco, and the United States. He stayed and studied in Egypt and Turkey. Dr. Kumek, who remains interested in physics—solves physics problems to relax—enjoys different languages: German, Spanish, Arabic, Urdu, and Turkish, especially in his research of scriptural analysis. Dr. Kumek takes great pleasure in classical poetry as well.

ACKNOWLEDGMENTS

I would like to thank all my unnamed teachers, friends, and students for their input, ideas, suggestions, help, and support during and before the preparation of this book.

I would like to thank Dr. David Banks, faculty of the Department of Anthropology, State University of New York (SUNY) at Buffalo, for meeting with me daily to go over the manuscript. I would like to also thank Sister Umm Aisha al-Damisqhi, Br. Ali Rifat at-Turki, Sheikh Omar of Maryland al-Hindi, Br. Khalid al-Misri, Sheikh Tamer of Buffalo, Sheikh Ali of Hartford Seminary, and Sheikh Jaber Harris al-Amricani for all their editing and suggestions and comments. Lastly, I would like to thank all of my family members for their patience with me during the preparation of this book.

GLOSSARY

'Abd: the true lover and therefore, worshipper, bowing with love, respect, and gratitude for Allah

'Afw: Pardon, forgiveness.

'Afiyah: Spiritual and bodily well-being.

Akhirah: Afterlife

Al-Hayy: One of the Names and Attributes of Allah. One of the translations can be "the One Who is All-Alive and All-Active, the Source of all lives." This Name is considered as one of the greatest Names of Allah.

Al-Qayyum: One of the Names and Attributes of Allah. One of the translations can be "the One Who is All- Continuously Alive and Active without beginning and end, the Permanent and the Forever." This Name is considered as one of the greatest Names of Allah.

Alhamdulillah: All gratitude, thanks, appreciation truly belongs to Allah and fully credited to Allah

Allah (SWT): Allah سبحانه وتعالى. The expression سبحانه وتعالى read as Subhãnahu wa Tã'la also abbreviated as SWT and written as also Allah (SWT) is an expression of respect when the Name of Allah is mentioned. Among these expressions many English translations, one can be "Allah is One, Unique and Perfect with all the Divine Attributes and Names, far beyond human's negative and wrong constructions and imaginations. All Glory Belongs to Allah, the Most Exalted, the Most Respected, and the Most High."

Allah سبحانه وتعالى: The expression سبحانه وتعالى read as Subhãnahu wa Tã'la also abbreviated as SWT and written as also Allah (SWT) is an expression of respect when the Name of Allah is mentioned. Among these expressions many English translations, one can be "Allah is One, Unique and Perfect with all the Divine Attributes and Names, far beyond human's negative and wrong constructions and imaginations. All Glory Belongs to Allah, the Most Exalted, the Most Respected, and the Most High."

Allah: Proper Name of the One and Only Unique Creator, with other numerous Names and Attributes, translated in English as God.

Allahu A'lam: Allah knows the best

Allahu Akbar: Allah is always Greater, and the Most High. Allah is beyond and above all your implicit and explicit deities, fears, attachments, and shelters.

Allahumma Ja'alna Minhum: Oh Allah, make us from those!

Amal: actions

Amalu-salih: Good and virtuous actions accepted by Allah

Anbiya: Prophets

Astagfirullah: Oh Allah! Please forgive me!

Awliya: The people who are progressing in spiritual journeys and seeking constantly the pleasure of Allah

Awrad: Plural form of wird, means daily regular and habitual spiritual engagements.

Barakah: Blessings and easiness from Allah

Deen: Religion, the teachings about what Allah سبحانه وتعالى is pleased with (halal) and displeased with (haram).

Dua: Prayer (singular)

Duas: Prayers (plural)

Dunya: World, or worldly life

Fadl: Grace

Ghaflah: Spiritual heedlessness, forgetfulness, and carelessness.

Hamd: Gratitude and appreciation. This word is unique, only used for Allah to express gratitude, thankfulness and appreciation.

Hidayah: Guidance

Hikmah: Wisdom, especially all the practices of the Prophet Muhammad is referred as hikmah in its technical term.

Ijma: Consensus, it is the consensus of scholars as its technical term.

Ikhlas: Sincerity

Iman: Belief

Istighfar: Asking forgiveness

Istiqamah: Following the Divine Guidance incessantly and continuously

Jahannam: Hell

Jannah: Heaven

Jawami al-Kalim: Conciseness of speech. A few words with dense and convoluted means. This is a specific title given and used only for the Prophet Muhammad, Rasulullah ﷺ.

Jibril: Angel Gabriel

Khashyah: Respect for Allah

Khayr: Goodness, virtuous acts accepted by Allah

La hawla wa la quwwata illa billah: There is no strength, enablement, and power except with the enablement, by Allah سبحانه وتعالى

La ilaha illa Allah: Can be translated as "there is no deity or god except Allah." This is the creed of Islam called shahadah. Whoever believes in this, is considered Muslim even though the person may not proclaim his or her faith in public, because belief is between the individual and Allah in Islam.

Labbayk: *At Your service, and Your pleasure!*

Malaika: Angels

Masnun: The Prophetic, Sunnah.

Nafs: Ego or self. There is an untrained nafs called nafs-ammara. This nafs or ego can ride on the person like a horse. This ego can control the person and can make the person do evil. There are other types of nafs that the person can ride on their ego and this can then be called self instead of ego. This self can be in control of his or her ego partially or fully. In the quality and quantity of this control, there are different classifications and namings. These can be nafs-lawwamah, the blaming self with repentance and regret, nafs-mutmainnah, the happy self in their relationship with Allah, and nafs-radiyyah, the fully pleased and satisfied self in their relationship with Allah.

Ni'mah: Bounty and blessings

Niqmah: Disaster

Prophet: When it is used as "the Prophet ﷺ" that is the Prophet *Muhammad (peace and blessings be upon him). The Arabic writing* ﷺ is read as "Sallahu alayhi wa salllam" abbreviated as "saws" when the name of the Prophet Muhammad is mentioned. The expressions ﷺ or saws are expressions and phrases of blessings and peace for the Prophet Muhammad. They are also the expressions and phrases of blessings and peace used for the other Prophets of Allah such as Abraham, Moses, and Jesus and others.

Qalb: Heart, especially spiritual heart.

Qiyas: Analogy

Rabb: Another Name or Attribute for Allah, can be translated as Sustainer and Nourisher of all worlds, and universes

Rabbul A'lamin: Another Name or Attribute for Allah, can be translated as Sustainer and Nourisher of all worlds, and universes

Rahmah: Mercy

Rasulullah ﷺ: The word Rasulullah can be translated as "the Messenger or Prophet of Allah." Rasulullah in its usage is the Prophet *Muhammad (peace and blessings be upon him). The Arabic writing* ﷺ is read as "Sallalahu alayhi wa sallam" abbreviated as "saws" when the name of the Prophet Muhammad is mentioned. This expression practically and commonly translated as "*peace and blessings be upon him*". The expressions ﷺ or saws are expressions and phrases of blessings, peace and respect for the Prophet Muhammad when his name is mentioned. There are also the expressions and phrases of blessings and peace used for the other Prophets of Allah such as Abraham, Moses, and Jesus and others.

Ridah: Pleasure

Ruh: Soul

Rushd: Spiritual Maturity

Sabr: Patience

Sahabah: Generally translated as companions of the Prophet Muhammad (saw). The disciples of the Prophet Muhammad who spent time with the Prophet in his lifetime.

Sakhat: Displeasure

Salah: Five-times daily/regular prayers

Salam: Peace

Salawat: Expressions and phrases of blessings and peace for the Prophet Muhammad. It can be also the expressions and phrases of blessings and peace for the other Prophets of Allah such as Abraham, Moses, and Jesus.

Salihun: The righteous People

Shadah: La ilaha illa Allah (Muhammadan Rasulullah). This can be translated as "there is no deity or god except Allah and Muhammad is the messenger of Allah." This is the creed of Islam called shahadah. Whoever believes in this, is considered Muslim even though the person may not proclaim his or her faith in public, because belief is between the individual and Allah in Islam.

Sharr: Evil and bad renderings, engagements.

Shifa: Cure

Siratul-mustaqim: Being on straight path, meaning following the Divine Guidance incessantly and continuously

SubhanAllah: All the perfection and glory belongs to Allah. Allah is far beyond from all the negative, wrong, and imperfect constructions, imaginations, and thoughts of people. In Muslim language, people use this expression when they are amazed by something. It is preferred say "SubhanAllah" instead of "wow!" as a phrase of amazement.

Surah: Chapter

Tahajjud: Strongly suggested/practiced night prayers

Taqwa: Constant consciousness and awareness of Allah with love and attachment

Tawfiq: Help and Enablement of Allah for achieving the good and virtuous

Tawhid: Creed system of Oneness & Uniqueness of Allah

Tawwakkul: Reliance and Trust in Allah

Tazkiya: The process of constant spiritual cleaning of heart, soul, and mind. This is the technical name of the lifelong struggle of a person in the practice of spiritual cleaning of heart, soul and mind until one dies.

The Prophet: The Prophet *Muhammad (peace and blessings be upon him). The Arabic writing* ﷺ is read as "Sallahu alayhi wa salllam" abbreviated as "saws" when the name of the Prophet Muhammad is mentioned. The expressions ﷺ or saws are expressions and phrases of blessings and peace for the Prophet Muhammad. They are also the expressions and phrases of blessings and peace used for the other Prophets of Allah such as Abraham, Moses, and Jesus and others.

Ubudiyyah: One's true relationship with Allah as the Creator and creation through appreciation, dedication, and worship.

Usul: Methodology

Waswasa: Bad thoughts, temptations or evil inclinations.

Wird: Singular form of awrad, means daily regular and habitual spiritual engagements.

Zuhd: Abstinence, detachment from everything except Allah.

Zulm: Oppression

INDEX

U

V

W

Z

www.ingramcontent.com/pod-product-compliance
Lightning Source LLC
Chambersburg PA
CBHW021147090426
42740CB00008B/988
* 9 7 8 1 9 5 0 9 7 9 0 3 5 *